CONSTRUING THE CROSS

The Didsbury Lectures
Series Preface

The Didsbury Lectures, delivered annually at Nazarene Theological College, Manchester, are now a well-established feature on the theological calendar in Britain. The lectures are planned primarily for the academic and church community in Manchester but through their publication have reached a global readership.

The name "Didsbury Lectures" was chosen for its double significance. Didsbury is the location of Nazarene Theological College, but it was also the location of Didsbury College (sometimes known as Didsbury Wesleyan College), established in 1842 for training Wesleyan Methodist ministers.

The Didsbury Lectures were inaugurated in 1979 by Professor F. F. Bruce. He was followed annually by highly regarded scholars who established the series' standard. All have been notable for making high calibre scholarship accessible to interested and informed listeners.

The lectures give a platform for leading thinkers within the historic Christian faith to address topics of current relevance. While each lecturer is given freedom in choice of topic, the series is intended to address topics that traditionally would fall into the category of "Divinity." Beyond that, the college does not set parameters. Didsbury lecturers, in turn, have relished the privilege of engaging in the dialogue between church and academy.

Most Didsbury lecturers have been well-known scholars in the United Kingdom. From the start, the college envisaged the series as a means by which it could contribute to theological discourse between the church and the academic community more widely in Britain and abroad. The publication is an important part of fulfilling that goal. It remains the hope and prayer of the College that each volume will have a lasting and positive impact on the life of the church, and in the service of the gospel of Christ.

1979	Professor F. F. Bruce†	*Men and Movements in the Primitive Church*
1980	The Revd Professor I. Howard Marshall	*Last Supper and Lord's Supper*
1981	The Revd Professor James Atkinson†	*Martin Luther: Prophet to the Church Catholic*
1982	The Very Revd Professor T. F. Torrance†	*The Mediation of Christ*
1983	The Revd Professor C. K. Barrett†	*Church, Ministry and Sacraments in the New Testament*
1984	The Revd Dr A. R. G. Deasley	*The Shape of Qumran Theology*
1985	Dr Donald P. Guthrie†	*The Relevance of John's Apocalypse*
1986	Professor A. F. Walls	The Nineteenth-Century Missionary Movement**

Construing the Cross

Type, Sign, Symbol, Word, Action

THE DIDSBURY LECTURES 2014

FRANCES M. YOUNG

CASCADE *Books* · Eugene, Oregon

CONSTRUING THE CROSS:
Type, Sign, Symbol, Word, Action

Didsbury Lectures Series

Cascade Books
A Division of Wipf and Stock Publishers
199 W. 8th Ave., Suite 3
Eugene, OR 97401

www.wipfandstock.com

ISBN 13: 978-1-4982-2002-6

Cataloging-in-Publication data:

Young, Frances M. (Frances Margaret)

Construing the cross: type, sign, symbol, word, action / Frances M. Young.

Didsbury Lectures Series

xviii + 142 p. ; 23 cm. Includes bibliographical references and indexes.

ISBN 13: 978-1-4982-2002-6

1. Jesus Christ—Crucifixion. 2. Jesus Christ—Crucifixion—Art. 3. Theology of the cross. 4. Atonement—History of doctrines. 5. Redemption—Christianity. I. Series. II. Title.

BT453 BT265.3 Y68 2015

Manufactured in the U.S.A.

In Memoriam
my respected Wesleyan grandfathers
Rev. Ernest Marshall (1878–1957), who was born in Manchester;
Rev. Sidney A. Worrall (1880–1978), who trained at Didsbury College.

Contents

Preface

Three things have made it a special privilege for me to be invited to deliver the Didsbury lectures: (i) the distinguished list of previous lecturers, many of them Methodist, amongst whom I am honored to be numbered; (ii) the declared intention that the series should contribute to theological discourse between the church and the academic community, that having been a key element in my own call to ordination in the UK Methodist Church while continuing to teach at the University of Birmingham; (iii) the opportunity, given Nazarene history and my own Methodist lineage, to share with the wider Wesleyan family. This last consideration has prompted me to dedicate this volume to the memory of my grandfathers, both ordained in the Wesleyan Methodist Church in years prior to Methodist union in the UK in 1932.

By publishing here slightly fuller versions of the four lectures given October 27–30, 2014, I hope to convey my thanks publicly to the College both for the invitation and for the experience of interacting with my audience. The hospitality I received during my week's stay at the Nazarene Theological College and the lively interest taken in what I was presenting made my visit comfortable, memorable, and heart-warming. I was encouraged by the good fellowship, the evangelical commitment, the openness to historical exploration of Christianity on a much wider ecumenical canvass than our own tradition, and the level of critical engagement with theological scholarship. I am grateful, too, that the College agreed to my proposal to include in this volume an adaptation and enlargement of a paper delivered around the same time (November 7–8, 2014) at a conference at Heythrop College in London. That conference was entitled "'For Us and our Salvation': Girard's Mimetic Theory and the Doctrine of the Atonement." It was clear, therefore, that the subject-matter was bound to cohere with the topic I had chosen to address in the Didsbury lectures and that its inclusion as chapter 2 would enhance the coverage of this volume. My particular thanks are due to Kent Brower for facilitating all this behind the scenes, and Robin Parry for sterling assistance with the production of this book version. I am grateful too to the Rev. Dr. Andrew Teal, Chaplain, Pembroke College, Oxford, for compiling the Index to this volume, with the assistance of Chris Long.

Frances Young
December 2014.

List of Abbreviations

General

ACW	*Ancient Christian Writers*. New York: Newman Press.
ANCL	*Ante-Nicene Christian Library*. Edinburgh: T. & T. Clark.
CCL	*Corpus Christianorum Series Latina*.
CSEL	*Corpus Scriptorum Ecclesiasticorum Latinorum*. Vienna: Hoelder-Pichler-Tempsky.
ET	English translation.
FC	*Fathers of the Church*. Washington, DC: Catholic University of America Press.
GCS	*Greichischer Christlicher Schriftsteller*. Berlin: Akademie Verlag.
LCL	*Loeb Classical Library*. London: Heinemann / Cambridge: Harvard University Press.
NPNF	*Nicene and Post-Nicene Fathers*. London: Parker.
PG	*Patrologia Graeca*.
PTS	*Patristische Texte und Studien*. Berlin: De Gruyter.
SC	*Sources Chrétiennes*, Paris: Les Éditions du Cerf.

Patristic Texts

Cels.	Origen, *Contra Celsum*
Comm. in Io.	Cyril of Alexandria, *Commentarii in Evangelium Iohannem*
Cor.	Tertullian, *De Corona militis*
Demetr.	Cyprian, *Ad Demetrianum*
De Spir. S.	Basil, *De Spiritu Sancto*
Dial.	Justin, *Dialogus cum Tryphone*
Ep.	*Epistula*
Ep. Barn.	*Epistle of Barnabas*
Epid.	Irenaeus, *Epideixis tou apostolikou kērygmatos Demonstration of the Apostolic Preaching*
Haer.	Irenaeus, *Adversus haereses*
Hist. eccl.	Eusebius, *Historia ecclesiastica*
Hom. Lev.	Origen, *Homiliae in Leviticum*
HP	Ephrem, *Hymns on Paradise*
Marc.	Tertullian, *Adversus Marcionem*
Oct.	Minucius Felix, *Octavius*
Off.	Ambrose, *De officiis ministrorum*
Or.	Tertullian, *De oratione*
Orat.	Gregory of Nazianzen, *Oratio*
PP	Melito, *Peri Pascha*
Praescr.	Irenaeus, *De Praescriptione Haereticorum*
Princ.	Origen, *De Principiis*

Introduction

Thomas Noble, in his Didsbury lectures of 2012,[1] challenged the classic approach to expounding the atonement through "theories." Despite his critique, elements of those much debated theories remain at the heart of his discussion, though overlaying one another rather than cancelling each other out. A similar conflation I have essayed in some of my own explorations of atonement. In fact, the cross has been a perennial theme in my theological journey.

My doctoral thesis was entitled *Sacrificial Ideas in Greek Christian Writers from the New Testament to John Chrysostom*,[2] and it covered the way in which the early Christians rejected literal sacrifice yet saw both the cross and the Eucharist in sacrificial terms. A brief more popular version appeared as *Sacrifice and the Death of Christ*,[3] the outcome of some Lent lectures in a local church, which both encouraged me to present my research findings and provoked me into trying to say why this historical theology could be important for people today; continuing interest in this early book is proved by its reissue in 2009, nearly thirty-five years after its initial publication.

A few years later I was asked to write a Lent book for 1982 and produced the little volume entitled *Can These Dry Bones Live?*,[4] one feature of which was an account for the general reader of the three "theories" of

---

1. Published as *Holy Trinity, Holy People: The Theology of Christian Perfecting*. Eugene, OR: Cascade, 2013.

2. Submitted to the University of Cambridge in 1967; published in the Patristic Monograph series, no.5, Cambridge, MA: The Philadelphia Patristic Foundation, 1979.

3. Published in 1975 by SPCK (London) and Westminster Press (Philadelphia); reissued by Wipf and Stock (Eugene, Oregon) in 2009.

4. London: SCM, 1982, 1992.

atonement. Then a key argument of *The Making of the Creeds*,[5] published in 1991, was that soteriology (that is, the doctrine of salvation) was an implicit driving force in the arguments and debates that produced emerging Christian doctrine. Meanwhile, the significance of the cross in my struggle to understand how it was that my first-born son was "created" with profound learning disabilities, already hinted at in *Incarnation and Myth* (1979),[6] had become apparent in the two versions of *Face to Face*, published in 1985 and 1990.[7]

It is scarcely surprising, then, that my recent updated account of my son's life and vocation, *Arthur's Call: A Journey of Faith in the Face of Severe Learning Disability*,[8] includes a chapter on the cross; or that my attempt in retirement to offer a "systematic theology" integrating the various aspects of my personal, academic, and church life—*God's Presence: A Contemporary Recapitulation of Early Christianity*[9]—has a chapter that moves from patristic understanding of the cross to reflection on what that might mean for us. And all that without mentioning the various articles that have appeared over the years in journals, Festschriften. and other collections . . . .

So what more could I possibly have to say about the cross? Well, what I offer here is different, though it builds on all that previous work and in places draws from it. Over the period of my career the wider context of biblical studies and theological discussion has shifted substantially—from modernity to post-modernity; and my intellectual outlook has opened up beyond the strict parameters of the linguistic, historical, literary, and theological traditions of scholarship that formed me and my contemporaries. Besides, my long-standing engagement with the early fathers of the church has encouraged recognition that we are ourselves creatures of history, limited by the socio-cultural environment in which we think, just as they were. So this project was conceived as a way of trying to learn from earlier Christian cultures by reconsidering ways in which they construed the cross *before* "atonement theories" narrowed the categories. It both takes its genesis from study of the fathers and moves beyond; on the one hand, drawing on other periods and, on the other, developing some patristic insights further than the fathers ever could have done themselves.

---

5. London: SCM, 1991.

6. Edited by Michael Goulder. London: SCM, 1979.

7. London: Epworth, 1985; Edinburgh: T. & T. Clark, 1990.

8. London: SPCK, 2014.

9. Cambridge: Cambridge University Press, 2013.

What I want to pursue is best described as a move from theory to *theōria*, to use the underlying Greek term, a word meaning something like a "seeing through." So, by *theōria*, I mean a kind of insight or spiritual discernment that comes through imaginative engagement or storytelling, rather than literalizing exegesis; through liturgy and living, rather than legal transaction; through poetry and preaching, rather than rationalistic system. Not that I denigrate our God-given reason, nor the benefits of analysis, research, model-building, or theorizing. But I have come to recognize their potential narrowness, the need for a more holistic understanding of rationality, as well as a respect for the creaturely limitations of the human mind, its language, and conceptual capacity.[10]

In a way I take my cue from the fourth-century writer Ephrem the Syrian,[11] whose work will appear and reappear in the following pages. He not only did theology through poetic composition, but even spoke of two divine incarnations; first in limited human language in the words of Scripture, then in the limitations of flesh in Jesus. God speaking to us, he suggested, was like someone trying to teach a parrot to speak by placing a mirror over his face, so that the bird thought it was conversing with one of its own kind.[12] The language in which we speak of the infinite, transcendent God is never adequate, always allusive, suggestive, metaphorical, pointing beyond itself, and, as other fourth-century writers, Gregory of Nyssa and Gregory of Nazianzen, suggest, only able to get near its object by a multiplication of images overlaying each other and correcting each other. Insight into the saving mystery of God's presence in one who cried out in God-forsakenness on the cross requires similar multifarious meditations, as well as a willingness to embrace the possibility of truth in paradox. As with all theological enterprises, construing the cross demands the richness of Scripture, the suggestive wealth of ecclesial traditions, the plurality of experience in different socio-cultural environments, along with endeavors to make some rational sense of it all: in other words, the Wesleyan Quadrilateral of Scripture, tradition, reason, and experience.

What I have said so far implies more than I have spelt out fully. Let me reserve further discussion of presuppositions and methodology to the

---

10. See further *God's Presence* for the discussion in this paragraph, particularly Introduction and chapter 8.

11. See Brock, *The Luminous Eye: The Spiritual World Vision of St. Ephrem*—page numbers are given to the second edition (1992).

12. *Faith* 31.6–7, quoted in Brock, *The Luminous Eye*, 61–62.

concluding chapter, and first demonstrate what I mean by *theōria* through key examples, simply observing now that the "seeing through" I envisage bears some parallel to the way in which icons function in Eastern Orthodox churches. Icons have never been regarded as depictions or representations in some literal sense; rather they are signifiers, meant to draw the eyes towards another dimension, to provide material for contemplation, meditation, and reflection, opening up to the beyond. For as Paul indicates, "No eye has seen nor ear heard nor the human heart conceived what God has prepared for those who love him" (1 Cor 2:9). But we can learn to look with amazement.

1

Passover and Passion

A Christian Passover Liturgy

Passover appears as *Pascha* in Greek, a lone word (Hebrew *pesach*, Aramaic *pasha*) used alike for the feast, the lamb, and the meal. Melito of Sardis explained in the rediscovered *Peri Pascha*[1] that it gets its name from *paschein*—the Greek verb meaning "to suffer." That was, of course, a false etymology, confusing the Semitic term with the Greek root, but the frequency of this linguistic mistake in early Christianity helps us to understand how easy it was to associate the passion with the Passover.[2] According to Melito the "suffering one" is the true meaning of the Passover festival.

Melito is instructive in other ways too; but first, a few critical and explanatory notes. I just described his *Peri Pascha* as rediscovered. The text

---

1. Text and ET: *Melito of Sardis, On Pascha and Fragments*, edited by Stuart George Hall; ET: *Melito of Sardis. On Pascha*, translated by Alistair Stewart-Sykes; this is the translation quoted below.

2. Gregory Nazianzen corrects this mistake: "This great and venerable *Pascha* is called *Phaska* by the Hebrews in their own language; and the word means 'passing over.' Historically, from their flight and migration from Egypt into the land of Canaan; spiritually, from the progress and ascent from things below to things above and to the Land of Promise. . . . [S]ome people, supposing this to be the name for the holy Passion, and as a result Grecianising the word by altering Phi and Kappa into Pi and Chi, called the day *Pascha*. And custom took it up . . ." (*Orat.* 45.10). Quoted by MacKenzie, *Irenaeus' Demonstration of the Apostolic Preaching*, 144.

we now have came to light during the twentieth century, a long, complicated story, by which papyrus leaves from different libraries, other fragments, and versions were gradually put together in the 1930s and then an almost complete Greek copy was found in one of the Bodmer papyri and published in 1960. This copy and the Coptic version bear the name Melito. According to Polycrates, Bishop of Ephesus, quoted by Eusebius, the first historian of the church,[3] Melito was buried in Sardis and, like other church leaders of second-century Asia Minor, followed the Quartodeciman tradition[4] of celebrating the Pascha: after naming Melito as the climax of a list of seven, Polycrates wrote: "All these kept the 14th day of the month as the beginning of the Paschal festival, in accordance with the Gospel, in no way deviating from but following the rule of faith."

Towards the end of the second century, the Bishop of Rome, Victor, challenged the practice referred to. It appears that generally the Roman church distinguished the celebration of the resurrection on Easter Sunday from the commemoration of the crucifixion on the previous Friday, whereas the churches of Asia Minor, probably represented in Rome by immigrant communities, celebrated their Christian Passover on the same night as Jews held their festival. The text of *Peri Pascha*—sometimes treated as a homily, but very likely to be regarded as a Christian Passover Haggadah[5]—makes a dramatic correlation between Passover and passion, our present theme.

The text begins by noting that the scripture describing the Hebrew exodus has been read—how the sheep was sacrificed, the people saved, and Pharaoh overcome. This mystery of the *Pascha*, it states, is both new and old, eternal and provisional—old with respect to the law, new with respect to the Word; provisional with respect to the "type," yet everlasting through grace. The notion of "type" Melito explains later on in an important digression.[6] Any composition, he suggests, is preceded by a sketch or prototype, the draft or model is not the finished work, but indicates what is to be, just as a preliminary outline made in wax, clay, or wood represents the completed work, the statue or whatever, which is to be much bigger, stronger, and better. The type bears the likeness of the reality to come, but then becomes obsolete. What was once valuable becomes worthless. So, says Melito, the Lord's salvation was prefigured in the people of God, the gospel in the law;

---

3. Eusebius, *Hist. eccl.* 5.24.

4. The term Quartodeciman deriving from the Latin word for fourteen.

5. Stewart-Sykes, *The Lamb's High Feast*.

6. *Peri Pascha* (Stewart-Sykes translation, henceforth *PP*) 36–46.

but once the church and the gospel arose, the type was depleted, the law fulfilled, and they gave up their meaning to the gospel and the church.

Anticipating this explanation Melito introduces his perspective on Passover fulfilled in passion:

> . . . the slaughter of the sheep,
> and the sacrificial procession of the blood,
> and the writing of the law encompass Christ,
> on whose account everything in the previous law took place,
> though better in the new dispensation . . . .[7]

> For he was born a son,
> and led as a lamb,
> and slaughtered as a sheep,
> and buried as a man,
> and rose from the dead as God,
> being God by his nature and a man . . . .[8]

> He is son, in that he is begotten.
> He is sheep, in that he suffers.
> He is human, in that he is buried.
> He is God, in that he is raised up.
> This is Jesus the Christ,
> to whom be the glory for ever and ever. Amen.[9]

The next section is a dramatic rehearsal of the original exodus escape, based on Exodus 12, but free in its rhetorical development.

> "Look," he says, "you shall take a lamb, without spot or blemish,
> and, toward the evening, slaughter it with the sons of Israel.
> And eat it at night with haste.
> And not a bone of it, shall you break."[10]

He then specifies how it should be eaten and commemorated, and its blood then used to anoint the doors of the houses to avert the angel of death. Moses is described as performing "the mystery at night with the sons of

---

7. *PP* 6.
8. *PP* 8.
9. *PP* 9–10.
10. *PP* 12.

Israel," and then disaster strikes "those uninitiated in the mystery, those with no part in the *Pascha*, those not sealed with the blood." Clearly the commemoration of the *Pascha* is described in terms reminiscent of the mystery cults of the Greco-Roman world, a way of making the narrative liturgically powerful within Melito's contemporary culture. The consequences for Egypt are graphically imagined—the mourning and wailing, Pharaoh in sackcloth and ashes, surrounded by the people full of grief and woe. The firstborn cry out as they plunge into death, not only human sons, but firstborn calves and foals.

> It was a terrible spectacle to watch,
> the mothers of the Egyptians with hair undone,
> the fathers with minds undone,
> wailing terribly in the Egyptian tongue:
> "By evil chance we are bereaved in a moment of our firstborn issue."
> They were beating their breasts,
> they were tapping time with their hands for the dance of the dead.
>
> Such was the calamity which surrounded Egypt,
> and made her suddenly childless.
> Israel was guarded by the slaughter of the sheep,
> and was illuminated by the shedding of blood,
> and the death of the sheep was a wall for the people.
>
> Oh, strange and ineffable mystery!
> The slaughter of the sheep was Israel's salvation,
> and the death of the sheep was life for the people,
> and the blood averted the angel.[11]

Then Melito asks the angel what caused that aversion: was it the slaughter of the sheep or the life of the Lord, the death of the sheep or the type of the Lord? It is clear that the angel turned away because he saw "the mystery of the Lord in the sheep, the life of the Lord in the slaughter of the sheep, and the type of the Lord in the death of the sheep."[12] The reality to which the type pointed was what made it powerful for salvation. This is where he digresses to provide that explanation of type. What was once of value becomes worthless before its powerful fulfillment.

11. *PP* 29–31.

12. *PP* 32.

Now Melito shifts to the "proof" or demonstration of what that old narrative was all about—the mystery of the Pasch, the suffering one. He develops a parallel narrative,[13] an elucidation of the gospel. This narrative goes back behind the exodus, behind the call of Abraham, to the creation of heaven and earth and all that is in it. It tells of Eden, and the command to eat from all the trees in the garden, except the tree of knowledge. Capable of good or evil, humanity consented to the seductive counselor and broke the commandment, leaving as an inheritance to human children

> not purity but lust,
>
> not incorruption but decay,
>
> not honor but dishonor,
>
> not freedom but bondage,
>
> not sovereignty but tyranny,
>
> not life but death,
>
> not salvation but destruction.[14]

The narrative, paralleling Greek mythology as well as biblical history, then tells of catastrophic decline:

> The father took up sword against his son,
>
> and the son laid hands upon his father . . .
>
> And brother killed brother,
>
> and host harmed guest,
>
> and friend murdered friend,
>
> and man struck down man with a tyrannical right hand.
>
> Everyone became murderers,
>
> parricides,
>
> infanticides,
>
> fratricides, everyone on earth . . . .[15]

> Many other bizarre and most terrible and dissolute things
>
> took place among people:
>
> a father went to bed with his child,
>
> a son with his mother . . . .[16]

13. From *PP* 47ff.

14. *PP* 49.

15. *PP* 51.

16. *PP* 53.

> Sin rejoiced in all of this,
>
> working together with death . . . .
>
> Sin set his sign on everyone.
>
> And those on whom he etched his mark were doomed to death.[17]

But now the Lord made preparation for his own suffering, the mystery of the Lord being predicted by prophets and prefigured in types—Abel, Isaac, and others are listed as having suffered for the sake of Christ.

> And look at the sheep, slaughtered in the land of the Egypt, which saved Israel through its blood whilst Egypt was struck down.[18]

There follows a list of classic quotes from the prophets, including Isaiah 53: "Like a sheep he was led to slaughter and like a silent lamb before its shearer he does not open his mouth."[19]

The mystery of the *Pascha* is Christ. He is the one who comes from heaven and accepts the suffering of the suffering one, by wrapping himself in a body through a virgin womb, and suffering to set free the flesh from suffering. He is the one led like a lamb and slaughtered like a sheep, ransoming us as from the land of Egypt:

> This is the one who clad death in shame,
>
> and, as Moses did to Pharaoh,
>
> made the devil grieve . . . .
>
> This is the one who delivered us from slavery to freedom,
>
> from darkness into light,
>
> from death into life,
>
> from tyranny into an eternal Kingdom,
>
> and made us a new priesthood,
>
> and a people everlasting for himself.[20]

A number of rhetorical paragraphs follow, blaming Israel for this murder, for not perceiving the Lord who had chosen them and led them from Egypt. These make uncomfortable reading for ears sensitized by the Holocaust. But the climax is an invitation from Christ to all sinners to come and receive forgiveness.

17. *PP* 54.

18. *PP* 60.

19. *PP* 64.

20. *PP* 68.

So come all families of people,
adulterated with sin,
and receive forgiveness of sins.
For I am your freedom.
I am the Passover of salvation,
I am the lamb slaughtered for you,
I am your ransom,
I am your life,
I am your light,
I am your salvation,
I am your resurrection,
I am your King.
I shall raise you up by my right hand,
I will lead you to the heights of heaven,
there shall I show you the everlasting Father.[21]

The Christological centre of this whole parallel narrative is then further affirmed, becoming the climax of the whole.

Early Christian Reading of Scripture

So it is in this broad context of salvation that Passover becomes a typological prophecy of the passion, giving both meaning. Furthermore, what I have called the broad context of salvation is what gives narrative unity to the Scriptures, creating as it does the overarching parallel narrative needed for the type to work. The move from one narrative to the other is intriguing. Clearly what happened in the aftermath of cross and resurrection was a massive re-reading of the Scriptures. This not only led to the gathering of proof texts, but a fresh take on how the whole fitted together and illuminated God's purposes. To some extent we can see this anticipated in apocalyptic texts dating from around the turn of the eras (e.g., 2 Esdras), providing as they do overviews of biblical history, along with revelations as to where it is all heading. But the Christian focus is distinctive. Christ becomes the crux in such a way that the solution he provides to the ills of humankind becomes the key to the plight from which he rescues the human race. In describing the situation thus, I am influenced by E. P. Sanders'

21. *PP* 103.

groundbreaking re-reading of Paul, *Paul and Palestinian Judaism*: Romans appears to argue from plight to solution, but Sanders suggested that in practice Paul came to his understanding the other way round—it was the notion of salvation through Christ which led to the discernment of the plight from which rescue was needed. For Christian readers, looking back at Scripture from the vantage point of the cross, the story of Adam's fall became the clue to the salvation that the human race required. As Melito spelt this out, Pharaoh represented the seducer and Egypt the realm of sin and death, deliverance from which constituted salvation. Paul had provided the basic shape to this with his parallel between Adam and Christ; this, developed further by the second-century apologist Justin Martyr, became fundamental to the theology of Irenaeus.

To get a better sense of how the early Christian reading of Scripture was shaped by this, as well as how it affected understanding of the cross, let us turn to Irenaeus' work *On the Apostolic Preaching* (often known as the *Demonstration*). Irenaeus, sometimes designated the first theologian of the church, was Bishop of Lyon towards the end of the second century. *The Demonstration*, which survives only in an Armenian translation, is another rediscovered work, and has been described as the earliest straightforward overview of Christian teaching, as distinct from the piecemeal presentations of apologetic or homiletic works.[22] In the prologue, Irenaeus addresses one Marcianus, offering him a summary memorandum to strength his faith. He introduces one way leading to the kingdom of heaven, uniting humankind to God, others leading to death, and separating humanity from God. To take the first way requires holding to the faith received from the apostles.

The first article of faith is the one God, the Father, the Creator of all; the second is the Word of God, the Son of God, Christ Jesus, who, revealed by the prophets, in the last times became a man amongst men,[23] so as to recapitulate all things, to abolish death, to demonstrate life and effect communion between God and humankind; the third article is the Holy Spirit, through whom the prophets prophesied, and who in the last times was poured out in a new fashion on the human race, renewing humanity throughout the world to God. That, he says, is why the baptism of our rebirth takes place through these three articles: without the Spirit it is

22. See John Behr, Introduction to *St. Irenaeus of Lyon, On the Apostolic Preaching*, 7. This work is hereafter cited as *Epid.*, and John Behr's translation is quoted.

23. Here I follow Behr's ET. I am aware of the issues of inclusive language, but it is not always easy to render patristic rhetoric easily in English—in Greek they had the advantage of two words for "man," one meaning a male and the other a human being.

impossible to see the Word, and without the Son impossible to approach the Father.[24]

In expounding this further, Irenaeus finds himself creating a narrative so as to identify the God who is Father and Creator. The narrative describes God fashioning humankind in the image of God with God's own hands, and breathing the divine breath of life into him. Elsewhere,[25] Irenaeus makes it plain that those hands of God are the Word and Spirit through whom God created all things. This creature made "in our own image" was appointed lord of the earth, being, as image, God's representative, but placed in paradise to mature. There the Word of God would walk and talk with him teaching him righteousness.[26] Irenaeus insists on the immaturity of the man even before describing the fashioning of woman from Adam's rib; then he describes both as having an innocent and childlike mind, understanding nothing of "those things which are wickedly born in the soul through lust and shameful desires"; so "they were not ashamed," kissing and embracing each other in holiness as children.[27] Needless to say, the narrative goes on to tell how they disobeyed and ate of the tree of knowledge, losing their innocence. Irenaeus is clear that they were misled by an angel who had apostatized from God and came to be known as Satan or the devil. Humankind was banished from paradise.

The next section then selects a series of key incidents from the biblical record to show God preparing the way of salvation: Cain and Abel, Noah, Babel—these figure in a narrative of blessing as much as judgment on sin, and then Abraham becomes a model of faith, and Moses led God's people from slavery in Egypt.

> He saved the sons of Israel from this, revealing in a mystery the passion of Christ, by the slaughtering of the spotless lamb and by its blood given to be smeared on the houses of the Hebrews as a guard of invulnerability and the name of this mystery is the Pasch, source of liberation.[28]

The narrative moves through the desert, by Sinai, to the entry to the Promised Land, and then to the prophets who

---

24. *Epid.* 6–7.

25. In *Against Heresies* (cited hereafter as *Ad. Haer.*) IV, Preface; V.6.1, etc.

26. *Epid.* 12.

27. *Epid.* 14.

28. *Epid.* 25.

were made heralds of the revelation of our Lord Jesus Christ, the Son of God, announcing that his flesh would blossom from the seed of David, that he would be, according to the flesh, son of David, who was the son of Abraham, through a long succession, while, according to the Spirit, Son of God, being at first with the Father, born before all creation, and being revealed to all the world at the close of the age as man, "recapitulating all things" in himself, the Word of God, "things in heaven and things on earth."[29]

This is the cue for the climax that sheds light on all that has gone before:

So he united man with God and wrought a communion of God and man . . . . So, "the Word became flesh" that by means of the flesh which sin had mastered and seized and dominated, by this it might be abolished and no longer be in us. And for this reason, our Lord received that same embodiment as the first-formed that he might vanquish in Adam that which had struck us in Adam.[30]

Irenaeus now spells out the recapitulation motif in three points:[31]

(1) God had formed Adam from the virgin earth; so the Lord was born of a virgin, so as to demonstrate the likeness of embodiment to Adam, and that he might become the man "according to the image and likeness of God," as was written in the beginning.

(2) Through a disobedient virgin humankind fell and died; by means of a virgin who was obedient to the Word of God humanity was revived and received life. As Adam was recapitulated in Christ, so in Mary a virgin undid and destroyed the virginal disobedience by virginal obedience.

(3) "By means of the obedience by which he obeyed unto death hanging upon a tree, he undid the old disobedience occasioned by the tree." Irenaeus adds that since the Word of God invisibly pervades the whole creation—its length, breadth, height, and depth—so the Son of God was visibly crucified on a cross with those fourfold dimensions, inviting the dispersed from all sides, heights, depths, length, and breadth, to knowledge of the Father. The very shape of the cross takes on a salvific function.

The narrative is now rounded off, with demonstration of how the promises to Abraham and David were fulfilled, affirmation of the reality of the birth and death of the Son of God as a human being (otherwise that recapitulation would never have been accomplished), and summary of this

29. *Epid.* 30.
30. *Epid.* 31.
31. *Epid.* 32–34.

overview of law, prophets, and apostles as the teaching of the church. The second half of the work[32] provides proof of all this, showing how it was all predicted by the prophets, then accomplished as previously proclaimed: texts are quoted from what Irenaeus dubbed the "Old Testament" to prove Christ's pre-existence and birth of a virgin, then his healings and miracles, then that the passion was all part of the plan foretold, as was the Lord's resurrection and ascension; then prophecies of the apostolic preaching are offered, along with the calling of a new people of God from among the Gentiles.

Looking back over that summary, let me highlight a few points:[33]

1. The overarching narrative is about reuniting God and humanity in the person of Jesus Christ, who is the one human being truly in God's image, as well as God's Word.

2. This reunion requires the recapitulation and reversal of the story of Adam and Eve, so as to liberate humanity from sin and death, and finally recreate humankind in God's image and likeness.

3. Though hardly highlighted in Irenaeus' overall presentation, it is nevertheless clear that the Paschal mystery encapsulates this big story in the narrative of Passover and exodus, the blood of Christ protecting the new people of God from the angel of death and enabling liberation.

4. This is all embedded in a reading of Scripture that finds there signs, symbols, and prophecies, many and various, while having an overview of what it is all about which derives from seeing whole and parts anew in the light of Jesus and the cross. Irenaeus basically demonstrates how the church did what Luke describes Jesus doing: "beginning with Moses and all the prophets, he interpreted to them in all the Scriptures the things concerning himself" (Luke 24:27). Elsewhere Irenaeus wrote:

> . . . if anyone, therefore, reads the scriptures with attention, he will find in them an account of Christ. . . . For Christ is the treasure which was hid in a field[;] . . . the treasure hid in the scripture is Christ, since he was pointed out by means of types

---

32. Beginning at *Epid.* 43.

33. These points could be substantiated further by reference to the larger work of Irenaeus, *Against Heresies*; and see further my discussion in *God's Presence*.

11

> and parables. . . . [W]hen it is read by Christians, it is a trea-
> sure hid in a field but brought to light by the cross of Christ.[34]

5. The whole thing is the discernment of God's purposes from beginning
to end, in creation, in providence, in salvation, in the eschaton, purposes stemming from God's mercy and lovingkindness, and worked
out through God's very own Word and Spirit, who are, as it were, the
hands of God, executing God's divine intentions.

New Testament Precursors

So what Irenaeus has articulated here is the full picture already sketched by
Melito. What I want to suggest next is that there are precursors to all this in
the New Testament, though the whole typological drama is never explicitly
spelt out. In 1 Corinthians 5:7, for example, Paul refers to the Jewish practice of clearing out all the old yeast before Passover, "for Christ our Passover
is sacrificed for us." For Paul, the old yeast is sin, and it is important to
celebrate the feast with the unleavened bread of purity and truth. In the
Pauline Epistles this is one among a wide variety of types and metaphors
suggestive of how the cross is to be construed; and little is made of the story
here: neither lamb nor blood nor meal is mentioned. Other New Testament
texts offer similar hints. The pivotal vision in the book of Revelation is the
Lamb slain. The Synoptics indicate the Passover associations of the Last
Supper and the institution of the Eucharist, as does Paul in 1 Corinthians
11.23ff; while Hebrews makes much of Psalm 95, particularly its summary
of the desert wanderings, warning Christians against succumbing to parallel temptations to give up or rebel, and so never enter the rest—all within
the context of affirming that the suffering of Jesus took place for the liberation of those who were slaves to death. The Gospel of John, however, is the
work that most consistently produces a typological reading parallel to that
of Melito, though it tells us nothing about Adam and relatively little about
sin. Its way of featuring the passion as a new Passover, however, implies
the whole set of assumptions articulated in Melito, the writings of Justin
Martyr and Irenaeus, later also to be drawn out in patristic commentaries
on John. Reading those second-century texts, I suggest, provides significant
backlighting on the way the earliest Christians came to celebrate the cross
despite the shame and disgrace, defeat and failure of crucifixion, if only

---

34. *Ad. Haer.* IV. 26.1 (as quoted by MacKenzie, *Irenaeus' Demonstration*, 60)

because these texts articulate explicitly things implicit in the New Testament. This is notably the case with respect to John's Gospel.

It has often been noted that the difference in the way that John and the Synoptics date the Last Supper and the crucifixion may relate to the different practices of commemorating the passion, which were highlighted by the Quartodeciman controversy. Be that as it may, the significance of Passover for construing the passion runs deep in the Johannine gospel. Let us start with the obvious points:

- John 18:28 explains that Jesus was taken to Pilate early in the morning after his arrest, but the Jewish authorities wouldn't go into his headquarters because they wanted to keep themselves ritually clean, so as to be able to eat the Passover meal. So the Passover was still to come—Jesus had not eaten it with his disciples the night before.

- John 19:14 specifies that Jesus' final appearance before Pilate happened around noon on the Day of Preparation. So the crucifixion took place that afternoon when the lambs were being sacrificed in the temple in preparation for the Passover meal that evening. Passover would begin at sundown. "Behold the Lamb of God," the words spoken by John the Baptist in John 1:29 and repeated in 1:36 are rather literally fulfilled.

- John 19:31 speaks of an especially holy Sabbath following, and the desire of the authorities to dispose of the bodies of the crucified before the Sabbath began. So the two crucified with Jesus had their legs broken, but not Jesus, who was already dead. This is specifically taken to fulfill a scripture that is quoted in 19:36: "Not one of his bones will be broken." The scripture quoted is Exodus 12:46 (cf. Num 9:12), a specific direction concerning the Passover lamb.

These references make it quite clear that the Last Supper in John's Gospel is not a Passover meal—indeed, the story is introduced as happening on the day before the Passover festival (John 13:1), and the principal event of the supper is the foot-washing. All the Gospels report that Judas' betrayal was predicted at the meal, and Paul's account in 1 Corinthians 11 begins, "On the night in which he was betrayed" (v. 23); John alone omits what we know as the Institution of the Eucharist. That is doubtless significant, implying anxiety about the question how a Christian Passover could be celebrated prior to the sacrifice of the Lamb of God: the followers of Jesus would eat Passover after his death. John's Gospel took an earlier opportunity to discuss what is at stake in eating the flesh of the Son of Man and drinking his blood, a very stark and shocking way of describing Christian practice.

So let us go back to chapter 6: it is near the time of Passover again, and crowds are following Jesus. The issue of how to feed the large crowd is resolved by Jesus' multiplication of a boy's five barley loaves and two fish. Jesus withdraws and reappears walking on the sea. Eventually the story moves into a long, sometimes argumentative, discourse, as so often in this gospel. The people haven't grasped the significance of the sign, and want a better demonstration: "our ancestors ate manna in the desert; as Scripture says, he gave them bread from heaven to eat" (John 6:31). Jesus indicates that the true bread from heaven is the one who came down and gives life to the world. When they demand this bread, he says, "I am the bread of life" (John 6:35), and anticipates their refusal to grasp this. He goes on to state that those ancestors who ate manna in the desert died (John 6:49), but if anyone eats the living bread from heaven, he will live forever; and identifies this bread with his flesh. Each stage of the discourse meets with increased opposition, and now Jesus introduces something much more shocking— not only eating his flesh, but drinking his blood, an idea touching deep taboos in the Jewish law: "Those who eat my flesh and drink my blood have eternal life, and I will raise them up on the last day; for my flesh is true food and my blood is true drink" (6:54–55). This is a dividing moment: many followers turn aside.

So here is John's eucharistic discourse, associating the miraculous manna with the feeding of the multitude around Passover time. But note the layers of insight that meld into one another. Some kind of new exodus is taking place, and the manna in the desert models the bread of life given to sustain this new journey through the wilderness. Yet this bread is also the Passover—the eucharistic commemoration of the sacrifice that enabled escape from slavery and offered new life, the life of the age to come. Let me add three observations:

- In some rabbinic texts the manna in the desert is associated with Passover; so the link may well have been traditional.[35]

- In more than one gospel, the feeding stories are associated with Jesus' walking on the water. The escape by means of the miraculous Red Sea crossing might bear on this curious association.

---

35. See Stewart-Sykes, *The Lamb's High Feast.*

- Though immediately deriving from eucharistic practice, the introduction of the blood suggests further Passover associations. The blood of the Lamb had a specific function in protecting the people who were sharing the meal before their departure; for that reason, the doorpost and lintels would soon become a type of cross, and the blood would be associated with the seal of baptism.[36]

Maybe it is worth noticing too that, according to John 2:30, it was also around Passover that Jesus cleansed the temple and, in response to challenge, said, "Destroy this temple, and in three days I will raise it up" (John 2:19). Then, without specific explanation, the text suggests that he spoke of his body. The Gospel will go on to show, however, how that body was sacrificed as Passover lamb, may be consumed as bread from heaven, and may become the resurrection and the life for those who believe in him.

Nor are these the only places where John's symbolism draws on the exodus paradigm. Three times we find quite puzzling references to Christ being lifted up. Sometimes on first sight one might imagine a reference to ascension: e.g., 12:32, "When I am lifted up from the earth I will draw everyone to me." But the following verse states that Jesus was indicating what death he was to die. And in 8:28 Jesus is addressing the Jewish authorities when he says, "When you lift up the Son of Man." "Lifting up" must refer to the crucifixion, and in fact, the clue to its meaning is found earlier in 3:14, where another allusion to an exodus narrative is made: "Just as Moses lifted up the serpent in the wilderness, so must the Son of Man be lifted up, that whoever believes in him may have eternal life." The bronze serpent was lifted up as an antidote to snakebite, and brought healing and life to those dying in the desert.[37]

For John's Gospel, then, salvation through the cross of Christ is modeled on the stories of Passover and exodus. However, one aspect of John's text exegetes have often thought puzzling: the Passover sacrifice was not a sin-offering, so why does John read, "Behold, the Lamb of God who takes away the sin of the world"?[38] Now, we may discern how Melito's parallel overarching narrative might supply the answer, though clearly it is implicit

36. Daniélou, *The Theology of Jewish Christianity*, 273, referring to Justin, *Dialogue* CXI.4.

37. See further, chapter 4 below.

38. See discussion in commentaries, e.g. C. K. Barrett's commentary (2nd edition, London: SPCK, 1978); lambs are generally not mentioned as potential sin-offerings: bulls, sheep and goats, doves, etc. are to be used according to Leviticus. Most commentators seem to appeal to Isaiah 53 to make the connection.

rather than explicit. Salvation from sin is modeled by the escape from Egypt; as the Passover lamb protected the Israelites from the angel of death, so humanity is saved from sin and protected from its consequence, death, by the Lamb of God slain before the foundation of the world. It is a liberation, not from literal slavery and oppression, but from spiritual oppression, slavery to sin and death. Such themes, articulated more fully in Melito's *Peri Pascha* as human liberation from sin and death through the death of Christ, the Lamb of God, on the cross, would pervade Paschal homilies throughout the early centuries.

Passover, Passion, and Eucharist in Early Christianity

And so it is that in the fifth century, the story of Adam gets imported into his *Commentary on John* by Cyril, the patriarch of Alexandria.[39] Cyril was a pivotal figure in the Christological controversies from which emerged the classic Chalcedonian definition of the person of Christ. He wrote his commentary before getting involved in the dispute with Nestorius, but already we can see his characteristic emphasis on the incarnation of the Son of God. "The Word became flesh" in order to restore what was lost: "It was necessary for the affected part to obtain release from evil. . . . It was necessary that when the flesh had become his own flesh, it should partake of his own immortality."

Cyril notes that fire has the power to transfer to wood the physical quality of its energy, and it would be absurd not to assume that the Word of God could make his life operative in the flesh. The Word dwelling in flesh reveals a deep mystery: "For we were all in Christ. The common element is summed up in his person, which is also why he was called the last Adam: he enriched our common nature with everything conducive to joy and glory, just as the first Adam impoverished it with everything bringing corruption and gloom."

Given Cyril's role in the Christological controversies, it is tempting to consign much of what he says to that context. Yet ultimately his thought is rooted in the typological traditions we have been exploring and their celebration in liturgy. A prime concern for Cyril is "the eucharistic reception of the holy flesh and blood which restores man wholly to incorruption . . . ."

39. The following extracts are quoted from Norman Russell, *Cyril of Alexandria*, 96–109.

"The holy body of Christ endows those who receive it with life, and keeps us incorrupt when it is mingled with our bodies."

This is developed a lot further when Cyril reaches John chapter 6: "For those who do not receive Jesus through the sacrament will continue to live utterly bereft of any share in the life of holiness and blessedness. . . . And his holy body is no less life-giving, for it has been constituted in some way and ineffably united with the Word that gives life to all things." A few paragraphs later he grounds this in the Passover story:

> Is it not obvious to everyone that when in obedience to the divine law they sacrificed the lamb, and having tasted of its flesh anointed the doorpost with blood, death was forced to pass them by as a sanctified people (cf. Exod 12:7)? For the destroyer, that is the death of the flesh, was arrayed against the whole of humanity on account of the transgression of our original ancestor. . . . But since Christ was going to overthrow this terrible tyrant by coming to be in us as Life through his holy flesh, the mystery was prefigured to those who lived long ago, and they tasted of the flesh of the lamb, and sanctified by the blood were saved, for he who was set to destroy them passed by, in accordance with the will of God, since they were partakers of the lamb.

Clearly Cyril has an incarnational rather than cross-centered view of salvation. Yet it is grounded in the eucharistic sacrament, and the Passover/passion typology still shapes the overall picture. Furthermore, it requires the death or sacrifice of the body of Christ so that it is made available as food for eternal life. One is reminded of that phrase used of the Eucharist by Ignatius of Antioch in the early second century, before Melito or any of the others explored here so far: "the medicine of immortality, and the sovereign remedy by which we escape death and live in Jesus Christ for evermore."[40] Furthermore, Cyril's discussion of the Eucharist, together with Melito's text with which we began, suggest that the space wherein this typological insight (*theōria*) into the link between Passover and passion could be generated was provided by the commemorative meal, the body given, the blood shed, and the Scripture read. In that context, the community was drawn into the story—both stories: the Passover/exodus narrative and the big overarching saga of God's creative engagement with creatures endowed with God's image. The remembrance, as often in John's Gospel, is a way of

40. Ignatius, *Ephesians* 20; ET here quoted is by Andrew Louth, *Early Christian Writings.*

grasping the import of the Scriptures, the events of the Gospel enabling typological understanding of the Old Testament.[41] So drawn into stories made real through the sacrament, the community made them its own, knew themselves as God's people, chosen and protected from the harms of sin and death by the blood of the Lamb, delivered from oppression and slavery to the world, the flesh, and the devil. The community's identity was framed through this commemoration of the Lamb of God dying at Passover, and this must surely have been the earliest construal of the meaning of the cross, remarkably associated, not with suffering, judgment, or penalty-paying, but with rejoicing in the saving grace and mercy of God, who provided the means of escape and the way to the land of promise.

Concluding Reflections

Let me briefly reflect on the principal discoveries made in this first exploration, and open up questions raised:

1. On Passover as the earliest way of construing the cross

The passion was construed in terms of the Passover in the context of early Christian commemorative liturgies, where the sharing of bread and wine meant proclaiming the Lord's death till he come, receiving life through his body given in death, and protection from his blood shed. It seems to have been in line with Jesus' own signification of the meaning of his death at the Last Supper. It is highly likely, given the Passover references in Paul and the Gospels, that this was the very first way in which the shame of the cross was turned into a focus of celebration.

2. On atonement theories

If we enquire how this relates to the usual atonement theories, we find it fits, to some extent, with Aulen's classic theory. There is an implied dualism, humanity seduced by a fallen angel, and then rescued from the consequences by God in Christ. But there is no trace of the idea of victory over the powers of evil in a cosmic battle, nor of a ransom offered to the devil to buy freedom for humankind. There is no attempt to produce a rational

41. Stewart-Sykes, *The Lamb's High Feast*, 51.

schema in terms of some kind of transaction. Rather, there is a collective experience of entering imaginatively into an ancient story, through commemoration, and finding self-knowledge, release, and enlightenment in the act of that liturgical and typological engagement with Scripture, read in the light of the cross of Christ. The basic insight is that the intended relationship between God and human creatures is restored—once again in communion, they are at-one-d.

3. On what it means to be a liberated community

The early Christian claim that Christ died for our sins seems first understood not in the way usually claimed by the evangelical "simple gospel." It is communal not individual, and refers back to Scripture's way of articulating the corporate failure of the whole of humanity in the story of Adam. It is conceived as escape from prison, liberation from slavery and oppression, not understood through the sacrificial system of the law, nor through a penal justice system. The blood gets its power from the way it subverted the angel of death, not from ideas about purification or atonement—in other words, from going back to the Passover story, not from making analogies with the ritual sacrifices in the temple. The effect of Christ dying for our sins is made real, not by being born again through an individual conversion experience, but through baptism and Eucharist. The word "seal," often used for baptism, alluded also to the blood that sealed the doorposts and protected the people. The sacraments together signified rebirth through dying and rising with Christ, followed by continual reception of his divine life through the eucharistic bread, so as to be incorporated into the new humanity, delivered from death through the power of his blood, and renewed through his incarnation.

This may be vividly illustrated by quoting from a fourth-century Easter sermon, preached in Cappadocia by Gregory Nazianzen:

> Yesterday, the lamb was slain, and the doorposts anointed and Egypt bewailed her firstborn, and the destroyer passed us over, and the seal was dreadful and reverend, and we were walled in with the precious blood. Today we have clean escaped from Egypt and from Pharaoh, and there is none to hinder us from keeping a feast to the Lord, our God—the feast of our Exodus; or from celebrating that fast, not in the old leaven of malice and wickedness, but in the unleavened bread of sincerity and truth. . . . Yesterday I

> was crucified with him; today I am glorified with him. .... Let us
> offer our selves, the possession most precious to God and most
> fitting. Let us give back to the Image what is made after the image.
> ... Let us know the power of the mystery, and for what Christ died.
> Let us become like Christ, since Christ became like us.[42]

The "I" in this passage is a corporate "I," as is the "I" in the Psalms—an expression of identity with the community.

The questions we face today, surely, are these:

- Could we ever transcend the culture of individualism, which, reinforced by consumerism and choice, drives our self-understanding, and contributes to the accepted emphasis on personal salvation?

- How do we recapture that sense of belonging to a community delivered from struggle and oppression, of commemorating a shared sense of liberation in sacramental feasting, of becoming part of something bigger than ourselves?

- What might we do with this double story of Passover? The post-modern state of mind, we're told, rejects grand narratives, and this, the earliest Christian understanding of the cross presupposes, as we have seen, the grandest of grand narratives—from creation to the end of the world, and to make it worse, it seems to depend on the literal, historical truth of Adam's disobedience. We may imaginatively recreate the story's past power over people, even recall its liberating significance for slaves in North America, as captured movingly in some of those old songs know as "Negro spirituals," but could we ever find a way of real self-identification with those protected and delivered—saved in other words—through the death of Christ, the Passover Lamb?

42. *Orat.* 1.3–5.

2

Scapegoat and Sacrifice

So far we have discovered that Passover was probably the very first type through which the cross was construed, and that it was essentially a commemorative meal. Yet by the time of Jesus the lambs for the Passover feast had to be sacrificed in the Jerusalem temple, just like any other sacrificial offering, and in early Christianity types of the cross were found in the entire sacrificial system detailed in Scripture. As a religion without sacrifice, early Christianity was unique in the ancient world, yet sacrificial ideas lay at its heart. My research career began with exploration of this aspect of early Christian theology;[1] after half a century I now return to the implications of construing the cross as a sacrifice.

Back then I was concerned about two things: (1) the reduction of the term "sacrifice" in our everyday parlance to mean no more than "giving up"; and (2) the way in which assumptions about the meaning of sacrifice falsely contributed to the dominant currency of the penal substitution theory of atonement—it was presumed that God had to exact a penalty for sin, that sacrifice was a way of placating God's anger, and that the sacrifice of Christ was the sacrifice to end all sacrifices. I was convinced that misunderstanding arose from the cultural fact that sacrifice is no longer an ordinary everyday practice in modern societies. A collection of essays published in 2013, entitled *Sacrifice and Modern Thought*,[2] opens with the assertion

1. Young, *Sacrificial Ideas in Greek Christian Writings* and Young, *Sacrifice and the Death of Christ*.

2. Edited by Julia Meszaros and Johannes Zachhüber.

that sacrifice without a doubt has become an obsession of modernity; that might seem to contradict my point, but surely it rather confirms it. Sacrifice became an obsession in the modern period because it is no longer an ordinary, everyday reality. It fascinates as a universal trait of primitive human societies, horrifies with its supposed violent origins in human sacrifice, and haunts fiction and film; while its predominant public usage is with respect to self-sacrifice for a cause, particularly commemoration of war dead.

The editors of that collection of essays, which spans a range of disciplines from anthropology to sociology, from psychology to literary criticism, identify several contributing factors driving the obsession they identify: (1) theological debates since the Reformation concerning the nature and legitimacy of sacrifice; (2) increasing awareness of other cultures where sacrifice is or was practiced, with both renewed engagement with classical antiquity and the discovery of new worlds across the globe; (3) the development of anthropological and sociological attempts to define and classify rites that appear to have once been a universal feature of human culture. To these one must surely add the substantial Freudian influence on the humanities and social sciences. Back in the 1960s all of these elements impinged on background reading for my thesis, but the interdisciplinary dialogue has become ever more insistent, amplified by the theories of Walter Burkert, René Girard, and others, as well as by the voice of feminist analyses, which associate sacrifice with patriarchy, oppression, and abuse. Indeed, what is noticeable is the modern focus on victims rather than on the practitioners.[3] All this has generated an ever-increasing literature on the subject; here we can only dip into a sample, keeping in mind our main aim—to reach an understanding of how sacrificial practices might assist in construing the cross.

Scapegoat

Scapegoating is a term that has entered common currency. What it implies was beautifully represented in a TV drama called *Judas Goat*,[4] broadcast in 1973 and summarized in *Sacrifice and the Death of Christ*[5] amongst my

3. Noted by Zachhüber, in Meszaros and Zachhüber (eds.), *Sacrifice and Modern Thought*, 5, 13, 24ff.

4. By Jeremy Burnham, broadcast in the UK on March 22, 1973, in the BBC *Menace* series.

5. Young, *Sacrifice and the Death of Christ*, 105–6, slightly abbreviated.

reflections on whether sacrificial rituals can mean anything in the context of modernity. I here reproduce my account of the play:

Half a dozen middle-aged executives are sent to an Outdoor Centre and subjected to a grueling week of physical exercises. They start with gymnastics, climbing up ropes and over obstacles; they go on to crossing roaring rivers, climbing vertical cliffs, and joining in long-distance treks over snow-covered mountain areas. The youngest and fittest of the group bounces in at the start and introduces himself as in the running for a directorship, which he is almost certain to get since he is the boss's son-in-law. Then it is revealed publicly that they're all from different branches of the same firm and all in competition for the same job. Out of their stunned reaction is born hostility to the boss's son-in-law, which gradually affects them all. They feel he has an unfair advantage, he consistently shows up better in all the exercises—indeed, he alienates the entire group, and becomes "accident-prone." It is not for nothing that the director of the Outdoor Centre began to get alarmed. The accidents were unlikely to be accidents: the rope held safely for all the others, but broke as *he* crossed the river, sweeping him downstream in a dangerous current; on a perfectly safe, clean cliff, a boulder came loose and descended, striking *him* on the shoulder. The more he helped out others in difficulties, the more the bitterness increased. The tense atmosphere grew until eventually, by mutual consent, an emergency was developed in which he was "accidentally" killed—for we watched the boots pressed on his hands and into his face to prevent him from climbing to safety! The fears and aggressions of each individual had been fed in the group situation and focused on one member of it, until collectively they did something to which no single individual could have brought him- or herself. The climax of the play was the revelation that the victim had been sent merely as a catalyst and was the one person who had no hope of the job at all.

My comment back then was that this play expressed dramatically the sort of thing observed among group therapists:[6] groups have a dynamic of their own, which is greater than that of the individuals of which they are made up. It illustrated the tendency for fear, frustration, insecurity, and compensating aggressions to be magnified in a group and focused on a "scapegoat," which is then banished from the community. I observed that

6. For the following discussion I acknowledged a debt to conversation with Michael Wilson and his Pastoral Studies students in the University of Birmingham.

something like this must lie behind the story of Jonah being cast into the sea to remove ill luck from the ship in which he was travelling. I acknowledged that in the Old Testament the "scapegoat" ritual of the Day of Atonement provided some parallel: fears and aggressions and associated guilt feelings were projected onto the "scapegoat," who was driven out of the community so as to remove the disruptive influence of these emotions. In the case of groups observed by modern psychotherapists, the "scapegoating" is unconscious, hostile, and dangerous to the community; in the case of the old ritual, a surrogate was provided, the situation to some extent being consciously accepted and resolved by ritualizing it or dramatizing it. Thus, the guilt caused by the presence of disruptive aggressions and fears was cancelled and the community able to survive.

At the time when I wrote all that I was unaware that scapegoating lies at the heart of Girard's theory of sacrifice.[7] Here I will concentrate on *I See Satan Fall like Lightning*, a work published at the turn of the millennium in which Girard explicitly applied his theory to the cross. Girard's basic idea is that human culture arises from mimetic desire—we see what others want and want it ourselves. Out of this arises jealousy and eventually violence.

> These rivalries, as they multiply, create a mimetic crisis, the war of *all against all*. The resulting violence of all against all would finally annihilate the community if it were not transformed in the end into a war of *all against one*, thanks to which the unity of the community is re-established.[8]

In these few sentences Girard summarizes the socio-psychological mechanism uncovered in his earlier work, so as to show how it can exegete the cross. The whole point is to recognize in the crucifixion what is typical, even banal. Satan casts out Satan (Mark 3:23). Girard explains:

> The Satan expelled is that one who foments and exasperates mimetic rivalries to the point of transforming the community into a furnace of scandals. The Satan who expels is the same furnace when it reaches the point of incandescence sufficient to set off the single victim mechanism.[9]

7. His first book, *Deceit, Desire and the Novel: Self and Other in Literary Structure* had appeared in English translation in 1965 (French original 1961); *Violence and the Sacred* would not appear until 1977 (French original 1972) and *The Scapegoat* not till 1986 (French original 1982).

8. Girard, *I See Satan*, 24.

9. Ibid., 34–35.

Everyone is united in ganging up on the victim they regard as responsible for the ills, Satan now being "the violent contagion that persuades the entire community, which has become unanimous, that the guilt is real." "The high priest Caiaphas refers to this mechanism when he says, 'It is better that one man die and that the whole nation not perish.' The four accounts of the crucifixion thus enable us to witness the unfolding of the working of the single victim mechanism."[10]

Girard further points out that Jesus' death had the pacifying effect expected—Pilate was afraid of a riot, but owing to the crucifixion it did not occur.

> The torture of a victim transforms the dangerous crowd into a public of ancient theatre or of modern film, as captivated by the bloody spectacle as our contemporaries are by the horrors of Hollywood. When spectators are satiated with that violence that Aristotle calls "cathartic"—whether real or imaginary it matters little—they all return peaceably to their homes to sleep the sleep of the just.[11]

This single victim mechanism is the anthropological substructure of the passion, and is Satan demythologized. In other words, Satan is not a personal being, but is real in the sense that he is assimilated to rivalistic contagion and its consequences.

Thus, for Girard, the scapegoat mechanism illuminates the dynamics of the crucifixion. Like Girard, I too had noted how Christ was scapegoated, becoming the one on whom the aggressions and frustrations of his contemporaries were focused. They ganged up to get rid of Jesus: his attitudes broke too many social conventions, upset the *status quo*, conjured up visions of disorder and chaos—consorting with publicans and sinners was dangerous and breaking the traditional rules was the thin end of the wedge. Something had to be done in the name of God and the established religious and political setup. They patched up a charge near enough the truth to get him condemned in the Roman courts—namely, that he was undermining the Empire by preaching about the kingdom of God. Ironically Pilate was induced to release a real guerrilla and condemn this mock-prince Jesus. So Jesus became the scapegoat, the focus of hostility, because he brought insecurity and anxiety. He was cast out of the community and murdered because of their frustrations and fears. In this historical sense, he was like

10. Ibid., 36.

11. Ibid., 37.

the "Judas Goat," and suffered because of the cruel and dangerous passions aroused.

Also like Girard, I had recognized that human beings are still driven by the same responses. Modern life, I suggested,[12] has obliterated the safety valve of ritualism. In the respectability of modern society we try to deny our aggression, guilt, and fears. In suppressing them we find unconscious outlets. True, not many of us have been involved in an "accidental" murder, but probably all of us have recollections of groups in which someone is made a scapegoat, one person forced to "carry the can" beyond what is reasonable or justifiable. The recognition and acceptance of these emotions and their *katharsis* or purification by ritual means might constitute a more healthy and constructive approach. Primitive rituals had a function to perform in society; so symbols from them might have continuing relevance. The cross of Christ could be such a symbol.

So for us the story of Christ's passion might become a dramatic or ritual way of dealing with the emotions we would like to repress and deny. The story exposes our complicity in the violence and sin of humankind, the group dynamic that catches up individuals and impels them to do things they would never do left to themselves. The crowd sings "Hosanna," then turns on him; one of the inner circle betrays; friends protest loyalty but fall asleep, then run away or deny. The victim is progressively isolated—even forsaken by God. This event is a *krisis*; not just a crisis, but a moment of judgment, which is what the Greek word *krisis* means, and as John's Gospel makes clear, such judgment happens unbeknownst to the guilty party. At the end of John 9, for example, the Pharisees ask if they are also blind, and Jesus replies: "If you were blind, you would not have sin. But now that you say, 'We see,' your sin remains." So, as Girard has perceptively indicated, the story of the cross lays bare the dark realities of the human condition and we come to see Christ present wherever school bullies operate, whenever staff in so-called care homes collude in abuse, whenever military personnel resort to torturing their captives through sadistic horseplay—Christ's victimization is banal, as Girard puts it, a perpetually horrifying possibility in human history too easily overlooked by optimistic, liberal humanism. People gang up to get rid of anyone weak, vulnerable, or just different. The cross exposes what Christians have called "original sin"—the only empirically demonstrable Christian doctrine, as I once heard someone say. Yet it is overlooked precisely because we remain unconscious of this flaw unless

12. Young, *Sacrifice and the Death of Christ*, 106–9.

it is exposed for judgment; so too is the power of our collective Satanic impulses. For Girard this exposure of the single victim mechanism is crucial.

Not that his scapegoat theory originally emerged from the Bible—the key examples are drawn from Greek literature and Freudian interpretation of Greek myths,[13] as becomes evident in Part Two of the book under review. And from the scapegoat models of Greek religion and mythology there is another dynamic Girard purports to uncover: "the same human groups that expel and massacre individuals . . . switch over to adoring them when they find they are calm and reconciled."[14] In other words, they project their fears onto the victim, and then their hopes. "Lynchings restore peace at the expense of the divinised victim," Girard states. But now, by means of a comparison between the Oedipus myth and the stories of Joseph, he develops a significant contrast between biblical tradition and the universal pattern he claims to have uncovered. While both display elements of the single victim mechanism, in the biblical narrative the victim is not treated as guilty—indeed, Joseph is neither demonized nor divinized but remains human and offers forgiveness, thus breaking the cycle. When we turn to the cross, Jesus is clearly presented as innocent, and again is not divinized by the mob that demonized him—rather a minority of dissidents ruptures the unanimity and so exposes "the illusory power of mimetic snowballing." "Only the Gospel revelation allows a coherent interpretation of myth and ritual,"[15] claims Girard. The divinity of Christ subverts false divinities:

> Against the mythic deities stands a God who does not emerge from the misunderstanding regarding victims, but who voluntarily assumes the role of the single victim and makes possible for the first time the full disclosure of the single victim mechanism.[16]

The cross of Christ restores all victims of the single victim mechanism,[17] and conquers by complete renunciation of violence.[18] It is for this reason that Girard earlier treated the Gospels as the key to the theory, rather than the Greek literary and mythic traditions that offer his clearest evidence.

13. For Freudian influence, see e.g., in Meszaros and Zachhüber (eds.), *Sacrifice and Modern Thought*, Jessica Frazier "From Slaughtered Lambs to Dedicated Lives: Sacrifice and Value-Bestowal," 102, and Gavin Food, "Sacrifice as Refusal," 119.

14. Girard, *I See Satan*, 66.

15. Ibid., 125.

16. Ibid., 130.

17. Ibid., 138.

18. Ibid., 140.

In his original theory, Girard rejected the sacrificial interpretation of the cross, and wanted to strengthen the difference between archaic sacrifice and Christianity. The Epistle to the Hebrews he treated as a relapse into sacrificial thinking. After 1995, however, he saw the cross as "a divine recapitulation of the scapegoat ritual in order to subvert it," exposing it for what it is and deconstructing pagan sacrifice.[19] The identification of this theory as grounded, not in the biblical material, but in pagan and supposedly universal sacrificial ideas, is important—it both illuminates his hermeneutical projections onto the material and differentiates it from the traditional Christian meanings carried by treating the cross as a sacrifice, as we shall see. Yet, for all that, Girard's theory clearly has purchase on the relevance of the cross for modern anxieties about violence. Furthermore, go back 2000 years or so and there are some uncanny resemblances to early Christian use of the scapegoat as a type to construe the cross.

The second-century *Epistle of Barnabas*[20] quotes from the Day of Atonement ritual in Leviticus 16 and describes the two goats to be brought, one for a burnt offering, the other to be accursed. At this point the author draws attention to the type of Jesus, and continues: "Spit on it all of you, pierce it with goads, and place the scarlet wool on its head, and thus let it be cast out into the desert." Here the author is not directly quoting Leviticus—in midrashic style his tradition has assimilated the scarlet wool from the red heifer ritual described in Numbers 19, while the spitting and goading was presumably suggested by the cursing, if not by the type of Christ—as we saw in chapter 1, the fulfillment of a type such as the Passover could reflect back on the original. Apropos the scapegoat type, these extra details become significant. The person who takes the goat into the wilderness is to put the scarlet wool on a thorn bush—implicit, surely, is a reference to the crown of thorns—and then the author notes that it is the accursed one who is crowned; for "then they will see him on that day with the long scarlet robe down to his feet and will say, Is not this the one we crucified and mocked and pierced and spat on?"

---

19. Paul Fiddes, "Sacrifice, Atonement, and Renewal," in Meszaros and Zachhüber (eds.), *Sacrifice and Modern Thought*, 56; cf. Wolfgang Palaver, "Sacrificial Cults as 'the Mysterious Centre of Every Religion': A Girardian Assessment of Aby Warburg's Theory of Religion," in ibid., 88–89. Girard himself states, "What Christianity conquers is the pagan way of organizing the world" (*I See Satan*, 139), implicitly acknowledging the single victim mechanism was derived from pagan sources.

20. *Epistle of Barnabas* VII.7–11.

There are some remarkable parallels here to Girard's insights: the typology of the *Epistle of Barnabas* has as its climax the moment when the perpetrators realize that the one they cursed, spat on, and pierced is the Son of God;[21] and the typology presumes the death of the victim. Has "Barnabas" read the Bible in light of Greek myths, just as Girard appears to have done?

For the Leviticus text on which the typology is based is different: the goat is not cursed, spat on, pierced, and banished, there is no blood and the goat is not killed—in Scripture the live goat is set free in the wilderness, a contrast noted by Origen as well as present readers.[22] Furthermore, it is not by an unconscious mechanism that violence is dealt with and peace restored; rather it is by a very self-conscious ritual whereby sins are acknowledged, laid on the goat, and dismissed. It is the other goat that is sacrificed. Nowhere else in the Old Testament is the scapegoat referred to, while in the New Testament the scapegoat typology is never employed—the Day of Atonement appears in Hebrews, but it is the sacrifices for sin and the blood rituals for purification that are associated with Christ's death on the cross, not the scapegoat. Just as *Barnabas* melds together biblical material, so Girard conflates scapegoat and sacrifice in a way never found in the biblical material—indeed he builds his entire theory of sacrifice on the scapegoat mechanism, seeing ritual sacrifices as deliberate repetitions of the violent process whereby purification and peace were originally achieved.

> Bloody sacrifices are attempts to repress or moderate the internal conflicts of primitive or archaic communities, and they do this by reproducing as exactly as possible, at the expense of the victim substituted for the original victim, a real act of violence that had occurred in the indeterminate past.... The proof that sacrifices are modelled after real acts of violence is that their fundamental structural features are always the same even if they differ in details. It is obviously the model of collective violence that inspires them.[23]

For all its positive and powerful insights, the scapegoat typology does not, I suggest, illuminate what it means to use *sacrificial* language of the cross—at

---

21. Cf. Justin, *Dial.* 40, where the two goats represent the two comings of Christ, one in humiliation the other in glory.

22. Lev 16:22. Origen identifies the scapegoat as Barabbas sent off *alive* with the sins of the people on his head, whereas Christ *died* as a sin-offering to cover the sins of those who were to be forgiven. (*Hom. Lev.* X.2.) Cf. Douglas, *Leviticus as Literature*, 248.

23. Girard, *I See Satan*, 78–79.

least not unless you buy Girard's theory that ritual sacrifices are deliberate repetitions of an original act of violence against a scapegoated victim. We need to consider sacrifice further.

Sacrifice

Girard acknowledges that from real sacrificers researchers have always got the same double response: "sacrifices were intended (1) to please the gods who had presented them to the community, and (2) to consolidate or restore, if need be, the order and peace of the community."[24] He suggests that "anthropologists have never taken them seriously," and that is "why they have never resolved the enigma of sacrifice." But he himself, while accepting that "the sacrificers were telling the truth as they understood it," proceeds to probe behind these straightforward statements to the hidden unconscious socio-psychological explanations already explored, thus assimilating sacrifice to scapegoating, creating a grand theory and falling into the same methodological trap that he attributes to others.[25] This is to oversimplify the complex reality of diverse sacrificial rituals and to devalue the expressed intentions behind them; it also flattens out the range of sacrificial practices in the biblical material and ignores the typological dynamics early Christians discerned in reading Scripture in light of the cross.

The issue remains: do we moderns really begin to understand what it meant, or means, to live a life where sacrifices are part of ordinary everyday practice, an unquestioned aspect of household, tribal, and civic life? Is it not all too plausible that we project our ideas back? I suggest two remedies: (1) careful attention to ancient texts written about sacrificial practices, whether critical, defensive, or regulatory, so as to discern ancient assumptions and rationalizations (and here I admit I'm re-validating my own work of fifty years ago); and (2) careful attention to actual fieldwork in all its complexity. The enormous variety of practices in the religions and cultures of the world means that "there is no single thing . . . that constitutes sacrifice,"[26] while recent comparative studies tend "to emphasise the ordinariness of most sacrifices" for "those who practice it," "embedded in the

---

24. Ibid., 78.

25. For Girard's methodological flaws, see Frazier, "From Slaughtered Lambs," 101, in Meszaros and Zachhüber (eds.), *Sacrifice and Modern Thought*.

26. Dunnill, *Sacrifice and the Body*, 6.

commonplace business of life"[27]—indeed, sacrifice is an action, something just done without discursive explanation,[28] a routine, which involves "interpreting life into a relation with the divinity."[29]

Now it would be impossible to survey all the relevant research, but hazarding an overview I will make the following observations:

- Looked at from an anthropological viewpoint, sacrifice had a lot more to do with food and its preparation than it had to do with communal violence.

- Looked at from the viewpoint of sacrificers, the practice had to do with maintaining relationship with the unseen powers that would or would not bless their lives with goods and necessities, especially food.

What this implies is that sacrifice was about the sanctity of life and the mysterious cycle whereby life is nourished through death[30]—for living creatures are entirely dependent for sustenance on the destruction and consumption of life and, in the case of humankind, preparing it to be eaten as food by plucking, grinding, dissecting, and cooking. Sacrifice acknowledges and sanctifies the death and violence involved in eating to stay alive; for every time we eat, something dies that we might live. Furthermore, dependence for life on life's ultimate source requires the acknowledgement, not only of the seriousness of taking it, but also of life's sheer giftedness, and so a refusal to take it for granted, the honoring of its provider(s), and the mutual sharing of its goodness.

Let me develop these observations further by reference to material I know from my own early research—biblical, early Christian, and other contemporaneous texts, along with more recent discussions of that material.

1. The importance of food and its preparation

When Deuteronomy insisted on the legitimacy of only one sanctuary, namely the temple at Jerusalem, it had to make provision for the secular slaughter of animals for meat (Deut 12:15ff.). Leviticus, by contrast,

---

27. Ibid., 10.

28. Ullucci, *The Christian Rejection of Animal Sacrifice*, 21–22.

29. Dunnill, *Sacrifice and the Body*, 10.

30. Cf. Flood, "Sacrifice as Refusal," in Meszaros and Zachhüber (eds.), *Sacrifice and Modern Thought*, 129: "Sacrifice . . . plays out the paradox of the affirmation of life through its destruction. Through death life is affirmed."

presumes that every time an animal is killed it is a sacrificial act to be carried out with the appropriate ritual. In pointing this out, Mary Douglas[31] notes that (i) care for animals is a feature of biblical provisions, especially Leviticus; and (ii) those creatures defined by apparently obscure rules as impure and unsuitable for sacrifice generally turn out to be wild animals or domesticated beasts of burden, while those which qualify as pure for sacrifice are unblemished specimens from the flocks and herds of a pastoral people, raised for their meat, milk, wool, or leather. Alongside animal sacrifice are other required offerings,[32] in particular the first fruits of every harvest—in other words, the rewards of agricultural labor, which will be gathered into barns for the sustenance of the people. It has also been observed that

> what is offered is not only always food, but it is uniformly offered
> . . . in *cooked* form. To make a cereal offering, the grain is ground
> into flour, mixed with other ingredients and baked; grapes are offered as wine, and olives as oil. Other items, like sheep and cattle,
> are presented raw and processed in the sacrificial rite itself, killed
> and made an "offering by fire" to Yahweh or by some other means
> cooked for consumption in a sacred feast.[33]

The instructions for sacrifice have three further significant features:

- they specify whether and by whom the meat is to be eaten for each rite they describe;

- they indicate exactly which parts of the animal are forbidden and dedicated for the altar and which are fit for human consumption;

- they make clear exactly how the animal is to be killed—a feature that survives for Jews and Moslems in the rules for *kosher* and *halal* meat.

All this we fail to understand because killing for meat is removed from our experience in abattoirs and governed by secular rules for humane slaughter. For people closer to the land, for whom killing for meat was a normal part of life—indeed, the culling of male young was inevitable to maintain the

---

31. Douglas, *Leviticus as Literature*, 89ff.

32. Cf. Frazier, 'From Slaughtered Lambs," in Meszaros and Zachhüber (eds.), *Sacrifice and Modern Thought*, 101: "The vast majority of sacrifices undertaken globally as a dedicated gift to a being with special religious status (i.e. a deity, spirit, ancestor, guru, saint or other guide such as a Buddha) are non-violent gifts in which the criterion for the offering is that it is something that most people would *value and enjoy*" (italics original).

33. Dunnill, *Sacrifice and the Body*, 36.

flocks and herds[34]—sacrificial ritual was a way of acknowledging the seriousness of taking any life ever, even for food. The taking of life was made possible by sacralizing it. This reinforced the sense of material dependence on the source of all life and of the nourishment on which it depended.

2. Ancient critiques of sacrifice[35]

As late as the second century CE, we find the satirist Lucian ridiculing popular notions of sacrifice in a somewhat lurid burlesque.[36] He questions the piety of those who think so meanly of god as to suppose that divine beings need anything from the hands of human beings, picturing the gods in heaven looking down and waiting for sacrifices to be offered. If a sacrifice is being performed, all mouths are open to feed on the smoke. Like flies they settle on the altar to drink up the trickling streams of blood. Now there was no point in mocking people for thinking they were feeding the gods if that was not in some sense what they took for granted. Many may have simply done what was customary without asking why, but the critique, however crude, implies an accepted connection between sacrifice and food. Of course, once articulated, people would see the absurdity of assuming that gods were dependent on humankind for food or pleasure.

Particularly telling is the debate among Neoplatonists of the third and fourth centuries CE. Porphyry[37] adopts the vegetarian position that the slaying of animals is morally wrong, suggesting that animal sacrifice originated in a time of famine when lack of crops drove people to seek other forms of food. He notes, as modern scholars have, that only edible animals are sacrificed, not snakes or apes, and females are ineligible because of their function in reproduction. He approves the offering of first-fruits, crops, honey, and wine. The simplest gifts can provide a feast for gods and human beings, and the more costly and supposedly better animal sacrifices are not only unnecessary but unworthy of the gods. Iamblichus,[38] on the other hand, defends the whole sacrificial system against Porphyry's critique. Accepting that it is inconceivable that the creator should leave superior beings

34. Douglas, *Leviticus as Literature*, 95.

35. See further my *Use of Sacrificial Ideas*, 24–34, and "The Idea of Sacrifice in Neoplatonic and Patristic Texts."

36. Lucian, *On Sacrifices* i and ix.

37. *De Abstinentia* II.

38. *De Mysteriis* V.

dependent on humankind for their food, and stressing the unsuitability for food of what is burnt on the altar, he offers an alternative explanation: sacrifice is a way by which lower orders of being ascend towards the higher, the whole universe working together and sacrificial rites reinforcing the common life and sympathetic union of all grades of being. Sacrifice witnesses, then, to the common creaturely origin of sacrificer and victim, and the creator is moved by it. The sacrificial fire is an imitator of divine fire, purifying what is offered and freeing it from the chains of matter; as the fire assimilates the sacrifice, so we are assimilated to the gods. This is, of course, an intellectualizing explanation, but interestingly confirms that sacrifice was about the life shared by all living beings.

From Socrates to the Neoplatonists, philosophers insisted that gifts must be worthy of the deity to whom they are offered, and holy sacrifices are offered by close contact with the divine and being transformed into the divine likeness. This takes us beyond the issue of food to the bigger matter of relationship, which is where the biblical prophets focused their critique:

> I have had enough of burnt offerings of rams,
>   and the fat of the beasts;
> I do not delight in the blood of bulls,
>   or of lambs, or of goats. . . .
> Learn to do good;
>   seek justice,
>   rescue the oppressed,
>   defend the orphan,
>   plead for the widow.
>   (Isa 1:11, 17)[39]

3. Sacrifice as worship

The Greek word *leitourgia*, from which we get "liturgy," meant the duties associated with holding public office—often burdensome and costly, since it meant providing the wherewithal for the maintenance of sacrificial offerings and public feasts in honor of the gods. Civic prosperity, in classical Athens for example, depended on such service. The worship of the Olympian gods involved gifts and banquets. In our own society, parties and gifts

---

39. Cf. Amos 5:21–24; Mic 6:6–8.

are associated with different moments or intentions: you may be expressing gratitude or offering an apology, or celebrating a birthday or a wedding, or commemorating an anniversary. In ancient societies such concrete social interactions also applied to relationship with the gods. As I put it in my early work on sacrifice, there were different types (kinds) of sacrifice: gift-offerings, communion-rites, sin-offerings. This is not to suggest a rigid framework—different rituals could be invested with different meanings, similar rituals with different meanings on different occasions, and there could be layers of meaning, articulated and unarticulated; but sacrifices, animal or otherwise, essentially smoothed and cemented reciprocal relations with a particular divine being.[40] The relationship was conceived in terms of client and patron, and was fostered by means of shared meals, or gifts offered in tribute or in return for protection. This was quite simply the only known way of worship. True, "apotropaeic" offerings of various kinds might be made to keep away sinister powers, especially by the more superstitious, but sacrifice, public and private, was about offering homage to the gods through gifts and shared feasts.

Paul's discussion in 1 Corinthians 10 assumes exactly that: you cannot share in feasts meant to honor the pagan gods or daemons without becoming their partners, thus dishonoring partnership in the table of the Lord. Among the people of Israel, he adds, those who eat what is offered in sacrifice share in the altar's service to God. If we now turn to the Hebrew Bible, we find there too that worship consists in gifts of foodstuffs and feasts, whether reading stories in biblical history books or examining legislation about sacrifice. Whole-burnt-offerings were made in thanksgiving or homage to honor God's goodness and greatness; but the vast majority of sacrifices were communion offerings in which people participated, sharing in communion with God, family, and community, feasting in God's presence on the rich food—for meat was by no means eaten every day.

Nevertheless, relations with Israel's God did create certain characteristic emphases: (i) Commemoration was particularly important. As we have seen, Passover was an annual commemorative meal celebrating the exodus from Egypt. Fertility rites were rejected, or transformed into reminders that

40. *Do ut des* (I give that you may give) was a tag often used in relation to Greek sacrifices, and taken to mean that they were like a business transaction or a bribe. I admit to following this in my thesis some half century ago, and it will be found in the reissued *Sacrifice and the Death of Christ*. This perspective should be modified in the light of a deeper understanding of reciprocity in certain kinds of relationships. See, e.g., Ullucci, *Christian Rejection*, 24ff.

everything was owed to God—the offering of first-fruits, for example, was to be accompanied by this statement:

> A wandering Aramaean was my ancestor; he went down into Egypt and lived there as an alien, few in number, and there he became a great nation, mighty and populous. When the Egyptians treated us harshly and afflicted us by imposing hard labor on us, we cried to the Lord, the God of our ancestors; the Lord heard our voice and saw our affliction, our toil, and our oppression. The Lord brought us out of Egypt with a mighty hand and an outstretched arm, with a terrifying display of power, and with signs and wonders; and he brought us into this place and gave us this land, a land flowing with milk and honey. So now I bring the first of the fruit of the ground that you, our Lord, have given me.
>
> (Deut 26:5b–10)

The person making the offering was then to set down the gift before "the Lord your God," and bow before "the Lord your God."

(ii) Recalling God's covenant with the people and ensuring its maintenance became the fundamental drive of the sacrificial system, which explains the increasing emphasis on sin-offerings and purification. God had said, "I shall be your God, and you shall be my people"; but God also said, "Be ye holy, for I am holy."[41] The Day of Atonement was an annual ritual for the purification of temple, altars, priests, and people, so as to ensure the maintenance of the holiness on which the covenant relationship depended. The blood rituals were highly developed, not only for that special day, but for all sacrifices, thus putting anxieties about impurity or contamination at the heart of the sacrificial system. But God was understood to be the source even of the means of atonement—in Leviticus, God says, "The life of the flesh is in the blood; and *I have given it to you* for making atonement for your lives on the altar; for, as life, it is the blood that makes atonement."[42] So the perception that sacrifice is fundamentally about relationship is reinforced by the biblical covenant with God. Furthermore, it is evidently not a transactional deal, but a response to the generosity and grace of God, the Source of every good gift, the Creator, the Saviour. The exclusivity of this relationship means that even traces of "apotropaeic rites" are modified. For example, (a) in the exodus story, the blood of the Passover lamb wards off the angel of death, but the Passover commemoration is focused on the

41. Douglas, *Leviticus as Literature*, 147–56.

42. Lev 17:11.

saving act of God; (b) the scapegoat is "for Azazel," perhaps once an evil or hostile spirit, but in the Day of Atonement ritual the goat just carries away sins, opening the way for sin-offerings to restore the reciprocal relationship with God established in the covenant. Covenant relationship, then, is the context for understanding the sacrificial rites elaborated within the Hebrew Bible.

It is this biblical perspective that should enable us to grasp how the crucifixion of Jesus Christ could become conceived in sacrificial terms. After all, it was not a bit like a sacrifice:[43] no officiating priest, no altar, no fire, no ritual slaying, dividing and apportioning of bodily parts, no blood manipulation, etc.[44] I have suggested that the catalyst for associating Christ's death with sacrifice was its Passover context. To put a complex discussion as succinctly as possible, it would seem that typological reading of Scripture was fundamental both to Jesus and his earliest interpreters. Passover was a feast commemorating the sacrifice and consumption of a lamb whose blood had kept away the angel of death; among Christians this was soon being replayed as a commemorative meal in which, rather than meat from the sacrificial lamb, the body of Christ was consumed in the form of bread, and in the form of wine his blood protected the participants from death—it was, as Ignatius would write early in the second century, "the medicine of immortality, an antidote to death."[45] Sacrifice had established the covenant between God and Abraham (Gen 15:5–20), and sacrificial blood had sealed the covenant between God and Moses (Exod 24:3–8); here was another covenant in blood fulfilling Jeremiah's prophecy of a new covenant (Jer 31:31ff). The commemoration of the sacrifice by which the new covenant was established and a new exodus made possible was a communal feast, a sharing of food, which was also, according to Irenaeus by the end of the second century, first-fruits offered and received in thanksgiving for creation.[46] Typology also accounts for the early affirmation that Christ died for our sins—for this new exodus was from the present evil age to a "new creation," and the new covenant meant the fulfillment of God's promise in Jeremiah's prophecy:

---

43. Zachhüber in Meszaros and Zachhüber (eds.), *Sacrifice and Modern Thought*, 18.

44. It should, however, be noted that already the death of martyrs was conceived in sacrificial terms, e.g. the Maccabaean literature (e.g., 2 Macc 7; 4 Macc 6).

45. Ignatius, *Ephesians* 20.

46. *Haer.* IV.17.5.

> I will put my law within them, and I will write it on their hearts; and I will be their God, and they shall be my people. No longer shall they teach one another, or say to each other, "Know the Lord," for they shall all know me, from the least of them to the greatest, says the Lord; for I will forgive their iniquity, and remember their sin no more.
>
> (Jer 31:33–34)

Under the old covenant God had provided the blood of sacrifice as a means of atonement—Hebrews 9:22 acknowledges this: "Under the law almost everything is purified with blood, and without shedding of blood there is no forgiveness of sins." But now, according to Paul, God had provided another *hilastērion*, a much debated word, but probably to be understood to as "a means of atonement" (Rom 3:25). So the Epistle to the Hebrews would explore the death of Christ as fulfilling and superseding both sin-offerings and Day of Atonement rite, providing a precedent for Origen's *Homilies on Leviticus* in which the whole sacrificial system is interpreted in terms either of Christ's sacrifice or of the sacrificial offerings made by Christians in response. As Origen would put it, "Each of us is our own whole-burnt offering, if we renounce everything and take up our cross and follow Christ, if we give our body to be burned, having charity, and follow the glory of martyrdom . . . ."[47]

Paul had earlier appealed to the Romans to "present your bodies as a living sacrifice, which is your spiritual worship" (Rom 12:1); the notion that self-offering is the mark of the supreme sacrifice must surely be modelled on the example of Christ.[48]

Concluding Reflections

1. On sacrificial offerings

Typology, I would claim, is the key to the way in which early Christianity conceived the cross as a sacrifice. So to understand the implications we need to grasp what sacrifice implied, not project back our own presuppositions. We have challenged here the modern idea that victims and violence

47. Origen, *Hom. Lev.* IX.9.

48. For the modern debate about self-sacrifice, see Pamela Sue Anderson, "Sacrifice as Self-destructive 'Love': Why Autonomy Should Still Matter to Feminists," 29–47, and Julia Meszaros, "Sacrifice and the Self," 66–82, in Meszaros and Zachhüber (eds.), *Sacrifice and Modern Thought*.

are primary for understanding sacrifice, and also the notion that scapegoating provides the clue to what sacrifice was all about. By implication this analysis also puts paid to the widespread modern assumption that animal sacrifice arose as a substitute for human sacrifice. Classical literature makes it clear that human sacrifice was an exceptional and extraordinary thing to which people very occasionally resorted under extreme duress. The story of Abraham's sacrifice of Isaac, or rather of the substituted sheep, may appear to lend the theory plausibility, but that is to make an exception become the rule and to read the story in light of the theory rather than attend exegetically to the text.

Modern readers have been tempted to treat the Abraham and Isaac story as a prime case of child abuse; but victims and violence are not the main focus of sacrifice. Furthermore, in context, the story is a test of loyalty, like the Eden narrative, this case being the more telling since, if carried out, the very act of obedience would *prima facie* prevent the fulfilment of God's promise to Abraham of descendants as numerous as the stars in the sky or grains of sand on the seashore. The story suggests that the most precious of God's gifts is what God demands; yet in the end, given Abraham's loyalty and trust, God provides what is required. Thus two significant points about biblical sacrifice become apparent: (i) the only offering worthy of God is what is most precious,[49] the gift of life itself, and (ii) the very things we have to offer come from God in the first place. This illuminates the New Testament emphasis on offering ourselves as living sacrifices, not to mention the saying of Jesus that "Whoever wants to save his life (soul or self) will lose it, but whoever loses it for my sake and the gospel will save it" (Mark 8:35). Nor is it surprising that the "binding of Isaac" became a key "type" of the cross: God the Father offering the life of the only Son so that eternal life might be available through his self-sacrifice. Biblical typology proves itself fundamental yet again.

2. On religious rituals

Ritual sacrifice is not just biblical. It appears to have been a universal practice in pre-modern societies, usually understood as concerned with survival and the relationship with super-human powers that granted and maintained life. Indeed, the secularization that has accompanied modernity may

---

49. Cf. Frazier, "From Slaughtered Lambs," in Meszaros and Zachhüber (eds.), *Sacrifice and Modern Thought*, 111.

have obliterated something once basic to human welfare. To place the cross in congruence with so fundamental a human practice was to capitalize on instinctive responses across cultural differences and to enable mission, but it was also to embed Christianity in the wider spectrum of religion.

Long ago I heard my New Testament Professor[50] argue that the Christian gospel is not a religion like other religions. Likewise, with different nuances at different stages in the development of his thinking, Girard distinguished Christianity from "archaic sacrifice." Yet what is absolutely clear is that, even though in the religious environment of antiquity Christianity appeared unique in its refusal of sacrifice, in fact it had a rich symbolic sense of sacrifice as the way to seal reciprocal relations with God and one another. This community of language and understanding would eventually facilitate the Christianization of the Roman world, and the continuation of sacrificial rites in sacramental liturgies.

Christianity has its own identity and characteristics, of course, but it may be worth asking how helpful it is to insist on distinctiveness in our world, where religion is largely dismissed as fantasy or accused of generating violence. It would perhaps seem more appropriate to explore commonalities with religions other than Christianity, and to affirm together the benefits to humanity of rites and beliefs that acknowledge life's sheer giftedness and, at their best, foster peace and participation, community and commitment, not to mention reverence and respect for creation as a whole and the mysterious divine source of life.

3. On atonement theories

Treating the death of Jesus Christ as a sacrifice enables a complex of meanings to attach themselves to the cross, none of them, I suggest, quite the same as any of the traditional atonement theories. The scapegoat typology could be seen as expressing something similar to the classic theory: if Azazel once stood for the devil, then the cross might be treated as an offering made to ransom sinners from a hostile power,[51] rather as the Passover sacrifice could be treated as an "apotropaeic" sacrifice to keep away the angel of death. But it is more fruitful to see the scapegoat type as pointing to the exposure of the dark side of humanity, along with its implicit judgment.

50. Professor C. F. D. Moule, University of Cambridge.

51. This is one way in which Origen read the story: *Hom. Lev.* IX.4–5; cf. *Princ.* III.2.1; *Cels.* VI.43.

The typology with Abraham's sacrifice of Isaac might be related to Abelardian theory—an extraordinary demonstration of God's love and loyalty to humankind, through the paradoxical picture of God offering rather than receiving sacrifice. As for Anselmian approaches, sacrifice was not some kind of transaction and had nothing to do with paying a penalty. It did have plenty to do with purification or expiation, and as in the Old Testament sacrifice was a God-given means of decontamination, so the sacrificial death of Christ could be treated as God-given provision of the means to eradicate impurity and restore holiness. Maybe this could be read as enabling some kind of reparation or payment of debts on our behalf. However, typological parallels suggest that the use of sacrificial imagery for cross and Eucharist had a lot more to do with establishing the promised new covenant, as well as commemorating it in a similar way to that in which once Passover had commemorated the saving act of God.

4. On katharsis

I have just used the language of purification and decontamination. Earlier Girard reminded us that Aristotle called the impact of tragic drama "cathartic," and *katharsis* means purification. Greek drama originated in religious ritual, and we already observed how the passion-narrative can function as a dramatic exposure of our complicity in communal violence. The sin-offerings of the Hebrew Bible were also about purification. Even if originating in acknowledgement of the need for sustenance to maintain life, sacrifices undoubtedly got invested with further layers of meaning, involving not just thanksgiving, worship, and communion, but also purification and atonement.

Christianity's approach to atonement has always tended to be moralizing and individualizing. Honor-shame cultures worry more about the impact of pollution on family or community: indeed, in the biblical world, deliberate sins led to exclusion and it was unconscious or inadvertent infringements of purity rules that were feared as causing contamination and threatening holiness. Such pollution needed detecting, then cleansing by expiation—concepts we might perhaps grasp better these days as pollution of the natural environment has made us more conscious of the issues surrounding contamination and purity. Somehow human complicity in the exploitation of the creation—both natural and human— has left everything stained, and a means of decontamination is desperately needed.

How might purification be achieved through ritual, whether by sacrifice or tragic drama? I have long found illuminating Mary Douglas' interpretation of the blood of sacrifice. In her book, *Purity and Danger*, she explains how primitive peoples took things that were taboo, like blood and death and, by putting these fearful things into a ritual context, sacralized them, transforming them from being life-denying to life-affirming: "The special kind of treatment which some religions accord to anomalies and abominations to make them powerful for good is like turning weeds and lawn cuttings into compost."[52] Such insight illuminates both sacrificial rituals and also the positive release experienced from the enactment on stage of the darkest aspects of the human condition in tragic drama—the very fact that they are exposed and faced, rather than suppressed, is purificatory and transformative.[53]

"Unless a grain of wheat falls into the earth and dies, it remains but a single grain; but if it dies, it bears much fruit" (John 12:24). With these words John's Gospel relates the death of Christ to the natural cycle of death and life. Compost, turning weeds into fertilizer, death into life, was the analogy Mary Douglas used to express the power of sacralizing the taboo substance "blood."[54] Earlier I used language about food preparation and consumption that implied that violence and destruction were inescapably part of the process. All these hints point to a paradoxical process whereby death and rot prove purifying and life-giving.

This model, applied alike to sacrifice, tragedy, and the cross, might bring together the alternative analysis of sacrifice offered in this chapter and the important insights we took from Girard's scapegoat theory. In her book *The Fragility of Goodness*, Martha Nussbaum mentions Burkert's theory that tragedy originated from sacrifice:[55] "The ceremony of animal sacrifice . . . expressed the awe and fear felt by this human community towards its own murderous possibilities." By ritually killing an animal and surrounding this killing "with a ceremony indicative of the killers' innocence and their respect for life," the sacrificers both acknowledged and distanced themselves from their potential for violence. "It is the work of tragedy, song of the

---

52. Douglas, *Purity and Danger*, 163.

53. See further my summary discussion in *Arthur's Call*, chapter 5; and my fuller treatment of tragedy in Young, "The Mark of the Nails."

54. See further chapter 5 for the way in which blood signifies both life and death in the Bible.

55. Nussbaum, *The Fragility of Goodness*, 37.

goat-sacrifice,[56] to continue and deepen this function of ritual by bringing the hidden threat to light . . . ."[57]

So to sum up: the association of the cross with the scapegoat helps to expose negative, indeed satanic, competitive drives—the human dynamics in which we are all complicit and which demand to be dealt with, while the cross as sacrifice offers both the God-given means of *katharsis* and the possibility of transformation through the creation of a community able to celebrate life, life being always sustained through death. Indeed, it seems that Christ's death on the cross is best construed as a sign of life, as will become even more apparent in the next chapter.

56. The Greek word *tragoedia* basically means "song of the goat-sacrifice."
57. Nussbaum, *The Fragility of Goodness*, 37.

3

Tree of Life

If Christ's death on the cross is best construed as a sign of life, then the ancient symbol of the tree of life must be one of the most important pointers to its meaning. The catalyst for my exploration of this symbol was preparing for a Palm Sunday service. On a recent visit to the original L'Arche community[1] at Trosly-Breuil in France I had bought a little cross at the workshop where core members of the community, those with learning disabilities, are employed. The white ceramic cross-shape, decorated with leaves and branches, was clearly a simple image of the cross as the tree of life (Fig. 1). Intending to wear it for the occasion I began to draw together images of the tree of life for a children's address in which Good Friday was connected with Palm Sunday.

---

1. The L'Arche communities were founded by Jean Vanier in the 1960s, and are now to be found in many parts of the world. Their basic principle is that people commit themselves, for a short period or lifelong, to sharing in community with those who have learning disabilities. Begun in a Roman Catholic environment they are grounded in a Christian ethos while open to all, ecumenical in many places, and in India multi-faith. See further chapter 3 of *Arthur's Call*.

FIGURE 1

From Eden to Golgotha

In chapter 1, though focused on Passover, we nevertheless observed how fundamental the story of Eden was to grasping the significance of the cross. We looked at the overarching understanding of the Scriptures to be found in Irenaeus, and his notion of recapitulation, as expounded in his *Demonstration of the Apostolic Preaching*: "By means of the obedience by which he obeyed unto death hanging on a tree, he undid the old disobedience occasioned by the tree."[2] This notion Irenaeus developed in his massive work, *Against Heresies*, seeking to undermine the false reading of Genesis promulgated by those who followed *gnōsis*—"knowledge falsely so-called."

The twentieth century rediscovery of gnostic texts has allowed us to reassess Irenaeus' hostile reports, but has also confirmed that many gnostics turned Genesis upside down: the serpent became the "instructor," the embodiment of wisdom, persuading Eve to seek knowledge and escape the clutches of the Archons (the rulers of this world) or the Demiurge, who had imprisoned their spiritual selves in the body and material existence. (See further, chapter 4.) As for the trees of paradise, the tree of knowledge and the tree of life, for some gnostics they were like the sun and moon, beautiful and vast, both with good fruit; indeed, the tree of knowledge, from which the first man ate, opened his mind.[3] For others, while the tree of knowledge was wisdom and light, from which the Archons tried to protect Adam, the

2. *Epid.* 34.
3. *Origin of the World*, in *The Nag Hammadi Library in English*, 169.

tree of this life was deceptive, and the fruits of paradise deadly poison with the promise of death.[4]

In reply, Irenaeus reaffirmed the identity of the Creator and the one true God, containing all things yet not contained, and asserted what strikes us as the more obvious canonical reading of Genesis: the issue is temptation, the challenge of obedience or disobedience, and "the knot of Eve's disobedience was loosed by the obedience of Mary."[5] Adam showed repentance, hiding himself, and so he was driven out of paradise and removed far from the tree of life, because God pitied him, for otherwise he would be a sinner forever and evil would be irremediable.[6] In other words, the exclusion from paradise was an act of God's mercy. But in Christ, the Word of God was united to Adam's human substance, and rendered humankind "living and perfect," so that, "as in the natural Adam we were all dead, so in the spiritual we may all be made alive."[7] Book V of the *Against Heresies* explores at length how death is swallowed up in victory, and God's handiwork perfected, according to the image and likeness of God, which is the incarnate Word. Resurrection and immortality are God's gifts of life to those "who have not life in themselves"; for "as the tree of life, so shall their days be," Irenaeus asserts, quoting Isaiah 65:22.[8]

Into this overall narrative Irenaeus inserts the passion: he did away with humankind's disobedience with regard to a tree by becoming "obedient even unto death, even death on the cross" (Phil 2:8)—in other words, by obedience shown on a tree.[9] Again quoting Paul, he speaks of fastening our debts to the cross (Col 2:14), so that, "as we were debtors to God by a tree, by a tree we might receive the remission of our debt."[10] He summed up everything by being made flesh and hanging on a tree, making a recapitulation of that disobedience which had occurred in connection with the tree through the obedience exhibited when hung on a tree.[11] And so the church is planted as a garden where we may eat of every tree.[12] I have, of course,

---

4. *Apocryphon of John*, in *The Nag Hammadi Library in English*, 110–11

5. *Haer.* III.22.

6. *Haer.* III.23.6.

7. *Haer.* V.1.3.

8. *Haer.* V.15.1. The Isaiah text follows the LXX version.

9. *Haer.* V.16.3.

10. *Haer.* V.17.3.

11. *Haer.* V.19.1.

12. *Haer.* V.20.2.

highlighted Irenaeus' references to trees, but two questions arise from this: First, why associate, even identify, the cross with a tree? And second, what is the relationship between the tree presented as a test of obedience and the tree of life to which Irenaeus refers elsewhere? He never quite clarifies this, but he can rely on a whole set of symbolic associations implicit in his cultural milieu, but which for us demand further explication.

The Cross as Tree

So first, why is the cross so easily associated with the tree? It is, of course, a move already made in the New Testament. The Greek word *xylon* basically means timber. It may sometimes be used for "tree," and appears in the Septuagint translation of Genesis for the trees in paradise. But more usually it is used for a stick or cudgel (e.g., "they came to Gethsemane with swords and clubs"—Mark 14.43), or a pole or post, or gibbet or gallows-tree, and so a Roman cross. The book of Acts twice (Acts 5:30 and 10:39) picks up the phrase "hanging on *xylon*" from its common use in the Greek Bible for execution by hanging (e.g., Gen 40:19; Josh 8:29; 10:26, etc.), using it for the crucifixion of Jesus (cf. also 1 Pet 2:24). It must have been a very early way of referring to the cross, since in Galatians Paul already makes an argument from passages in Deuteronomy about hanging and cursing. The passages in Deuteronomy read:

> When someone is convicted of a crime punishable by death and is executed, and you hang his body on a *xylon*, his corpse must not remain there all night upon the *xylon*; and you shall bury him that same day, for anyone hung on a *xylon* is under God's curse."
> (Deut 21:22–23)

> "Cursed be anyone who does not uphold the words of this law by observing them."
> (Deut 27:26)

Paul implies both passages when he writes:

> Christ redeemed us from the curse of the law by becoming a curse for us—for it is written, "Cursed be everyone who hangs on a *xylon*."
> (Gal 3:13)

He thus affirms that Christ bore the curse arising from failure to keep the law by bearing the curse brought on anyone who was hanged for a crime. Irenaeus' typology, offering parallel and contrast between the tree of Adam's disobedience and the tree/cross on which Christ was obedient unto death, makes sense against that background.

Typical of patristic imaginative associations is the exploitation of texts from right across Scripture that either contained the word *xylon* or related words or ideas so as to demonstrate their fulfillment in the cross of Christ. Justin's *Dialogue with Trypho* 86 provides instructive examples: Isaac carried his own "wood," as did Christ; Moses' "staff" parted the Red Sea and turned sweet the bitter waters of Marah; Aaron's "rod" blossomed; God appeared to Abraham from a "tree" at Mamre and comforted David with his "rod and staff"—so Christ redeemed the people by being crucified on a tree. Included in the list is Isaiah's prophecy that a "rod" would sprout from the stem of Jesse: in this case, cross and Christ seem identified. Indeed, the same identification is implied when Justin opens his list by suggesting that "this man, of whom the Scriptures declare he will come in glory after his crucifixion, was symbolised by the tree of life."

The Two Trees

So what about the *two* trees? This question leads us into more complex territory. It would seem that Irenaeus implies that Christ's obedience unto death on a tree reopens the gates to paradise and gives humankind access to the tree of life, but Irenaeus never notes the problem of those two trees, both in the midst of the garden. It is almost as though he identifies them, the tree of death becoming the tree of life through Christ's obedience. The same cannot be said about modern commentators. Since the late nineteenth century, it has been generally accepted that the tree of life did not belong to the original narrative. It appears in what many have judged to be a redactional addition—the expulsion narrative of Genesis 3:22–24:

> Then the Lord God said, "See, the man has become like one of us, knowing good and evil; and now, he might reach out his hand and take also from the tree of life, and eat, and live for ever"—therefore the Lord God sent him forth from the garden of Eden to till the ground from which he was taken. He drove out the man; and, at the east of the garden of Eden he placed cherubim, and a sword, flaming and turning to guard the way to the tree of life.

Prima facie these additional sentences shift the point of the story away from the acquisition of wisdom to that of immortality; furthermore, the story is complete without it—serpent and ground are already cursed and the man and woman condemned to hard labor. Besides this, no one is told anything about the tree of life when the couple are prohibited from eating from the tree of knowledge yet permitted all others (Gen 2:16–17); and Eve knows nothing of it when reporting the prohibition to the serpent, describing the forbidden tree as being in the midst of the garden (Gen 3:2–3)—all of which makes otiose for the core story, and therefore probably redactional, the only previous mention of the tree of life in 2:8. There both trees are described as being in the midst of the garden, though in a curious syntactical relationship, which only adds to the impression that the tree of life was an addition to the original sentence.

Of two recent studies, one takes this analysis as a given, the other seeks to reestablish the unity of the narrative. *Remembering Eden*, published in 2012 by Peter Thacker Lanfer,[13] is focused on the reception history of Genesis 3:22–24; observing various developments of this expulsion narrative in texts from Second Temple and rabbinic Judaism, as well as early Christianity, he does not hesitate to acknowledge redactional development before the Genesis text reached final form. By contrast, in 2007 Messinger's book *The Eden Narrative: A Literary and Religio-historical Study of Genesis 2–3* challenged the long-standing consensus. At the heart of the issue is the question of the two trees—the tree of knowledge and the tree of life, and the discussion is materially affected by parallels with other texts from the ancient Near East. Interestingly, the upshot of both studies is that the Genesis text comes from no mere picking-up of pieces from surrounding cultures: rather, widespread motifs and symbols found, for example, in the epic of Gilgamesh and the myth of Adapa are re-minted for a new religious context—even shaped as polemic in the redactional process. For in those ancient stories, while wisdom and immortality belong to the gods, humans are granted wisdom, but denied immortality; in Genesis, however, wisdom is seized by humans, and so life, the reward for obedience, is withheld. For Lanfer that constitutes polemic against knowledge or wisdom independent of the temple cult and the covenant with Israel's God. For Messinger, it is the clue to the basic theme and unity of the narrative—for the tree of life, a presence known to narrator and reader but not to the story's protagonists,

13. Cf. Anderson, *The Genesis of Perfection*, which is wider ranging and more readable.

emerges as the intended reward for obedience, missed because the test was failed. He thus takes the position put succinctly by Theodoret of Cyrus in the early fifth century in his *Questions on Genesis*: "Adam was set a trial with regard to the [tree of knowledge of good and evil], whereas the tree of life was proposed as his prize for keeping the commandment."[14]

That understanding, perhaps implicit in Irenaeus, is explicit in other early Christian discussions, and notably significant in the *Hymns on Paradise* of the Syrian poet, Ephrem.[15] For him, Adam and Eve were created neither mortal nor immortal; if they had been obedient, they would eventually have been allowed to eat from tree of knowledge, and then go on to receive fruit from the tree of life. In other words, they were created immature, not yet ready to eat of the tree of knowledge, and not even aware of the tree of life:

> Two Trees did God place
> > in Paradise,
> the Tree of Life
> > and that of Wisdom,
> a pair of blessed fountains,
> > source of every good;
> by means of this
> > glorious pair
> the human person can become
> > the likeness of God,
> endowed with immortal life
> > and wisdom that does not err.[16]

> For God would not grant him the crown
> > without some effort;
> he placed two crowns for Adam,
> > for which he was to strive,
> two Trees to provide crowns
> > if he were victorious.
> If only he had conquered
> > just for a moment,

14. Theodoret of Cyrus, *The Questions on the Octoteuch*, vol. 1, ET Robert C. Hill.

15. *St. Ephrem the Syrian, Hymns on Paradise*, ET Sebastian Brock (*HP* from hereon).

16. *HP* XII.15.

he would have eaten the one and lived,
>   eaten the other and gained knowledge;
> his life would have been protected from harm
>   and his wisdom would have been unshakeable.[17]

For Ephrem the two trees are not problematic because of the topography of paradise. Paradise is conceived as a mountain that tops every mountain; even the flood only reached its foothills.[18] The summit is reserved for God's presence;[19] and

> at the summit of that height
>   where dwells the glory,
> not even its symbol
>   can be depicted in man's thought.[20]

Yet there is the tree of life, "by its rays, the sun of Paradise," its leaves impressed with spiritual graces, and "in the breezes the other trees bow down as if in worship before that sovereign and leader of the trees"; whereas

> The tree that is called
>   the tree of knowledge
> symbolizes the gate
>   of Paradise:
> it is through the gate of knowledge
>   that one is able to enter in.[21]

The tree of knowledge is "hedged in with dread to serve as a boundary to the inner region of Paradise"—Adam was not to penetrate further beyond that tree.[22]

> The tree was to him
>   like a gate;
> its fruit was the veil
>   covering that hidden Tabernacle.

17. *HP* XII.17.
18. *HP* I.4.
19. *HP* II.11.
20. *HP* III.1.
21. *HP* XV.2.
22. *HP* III.3.

> Adam snatched the fruit,
>
>> casting aside the commandment.[23]

By the end of the third hymn, Ephrem draws a parallel between paradise and the Holy of Holies, with the inner part closed off. The hiddenness of the tree of life is thus accounted for. Elsewhere, Ephrem shows how it was revealed:

> Greatly saddened was the Tree of Life
> when it beheld Adam stolen away from it;
> it sank down into the virgin ground and was hidden
> —to burst forth and reappear on Golgotha;
> humanity, like birds that are chased,
> took refuge in it
> so that it might return them to their proper home.[24]

In other words, the tree of life re-emerges as the cross of Christ. In the paradise hymns Ephrem speaks of Adam resorting to fig leaves to clothe himself, and goes on:

> Then he came to that glorious
>> tree of the Cross,
> put on glory from it,
>> acquired radiance from it,
> heard from it the truth
>> that he would return to Eden once more.[25]

So the fair garden that God planted becomes the church:

> The assembly of saints
>> bears resemblance to Paradise:
> In it each day is plucked
>> the fruit of Him who gives life to all;
> in it, my brethren, is trodden.
>> the cluster of grapes, to be the Medicine of life.
>
> Among the saints none is naked,

23. *HP* III.13.

24. *Hymns on Virginity* XVI.10; as quoted by Brock in his introduction to *HP*, 60–61.

25. *HP* XII.10.

> for they have put on glory,
>> nor is any clad in those leaves
>>> or standing in shame,
>> for they have found, through our Lord,
>>> the robe that belongs to Adam and Eve.[26]

Paradise, then, has become the eschatological goal, anticipated among the saints, and celebrated in the rest of Ephrem's hymn cycle:

> Blessed is the sinner
>> who has received mercy there
>> and is deemed worthy to be given access
>>> to the environs of Paradise.[27]

Thus it is that Ephrem clarifies the Christian reading presumed by Irenaeus, and his picture of paradise is itself clarified by the reception history considered by Lanfer's survey of rabbinic and early Christian texts. For example, the Aramaic *Targum Neofiti* places one tree in the midst of the garden and one in the innermost part, thus resolving the Genesis text's ambiguities[28] and reflecting the same topography as Ephrem; nor can it be irrelevant that the Syriac Peshitta translation of Genesis 2:9 also puts the tree of life in the innermost part of paradise.[29] Indeed, Lanfer's wide-ranging discussion shows how, in many of the Christian and Jewish texts he explores, the tree of life "functions as a metaphor for blessing," or as a tree bearing "the fruits of immortality or healing"; but he also traces the way it becomes a multivalent symbol, employed as a representation of the temple, the faithful, the future Jerusalem, the Torah, or the presence of God. We will consider a brief selection of his examples, noting how they often emerge from the conflation of biblical passages.

The Tree of Life as Multi-valent Symbol

It was the Septuagint translation that added the "tree of life" to the Isaiah text that earlier we found quoted by Irenaeus (Isa 65:22). There is barely a mention of the tree of life in the Hebrew Bible outside the Eden narrative—the

26. *HP* VI.8–9.

27. *HP* X.13–14.

28. Cf. Lanfer, *Remembering Eden,* 44.

29. Cf. ibid., 51.

phrase occurs but four times in Proverbs, applied to wisdom (3:18), the fruit of the righteous (11:30), a gentle tongue (15:4), and, perhaps less pertinently, to desire fulfilled, by contrast with hope deferred which makes the heart sick (13:12). Yet all these texts would contribute to an association between the tree of life and the expectations of the righteous who study God's law; indeed, according to Psalm 1, the righteous are planted like trees by streams of water, which yield their fruit in its season, and their leaves do not wither, a picture picked up in the prophets (e.g., Isa 61:3). Christians find such images in Gospel verses about trees bearing good or bad fruit (e.g., Matt 7:17–20); and the Psalms of Solomon speak of "his holy ones" as trees of life, perhaps also calling them the paradise of the Lord, though the syntax is not clear: "Their planting is firmly rooted for ever; they shall not be uprooted as long as the heavens shall last, for Israel is the portion and inheritance of God."[30]

Thus, through the notion of the righteous being trees of life bearing good fruit, Eden becomes associated with Israel idealized, its righteous people never to be uprooted by exile again. The *Letter of Aristeas*, which famously describes the translation of the Hebrew Scriptures into Greek by seventy scholars, also depicts the land of Israel in Eden-like terms and Jerusalem as the holy mountain, gushing with rivers of water.[31] Expulsion from Eden began to parallel exile from the land promised and once occupied.

The *Targum Neofiti* makes explicit that obedience to Torah is the fundamental issue in the Genesis narrative: "If he keeps the commandments of the Torah and maintains its decree, he will live and stand like a tree of life for ever."[32] The Garden of Eden was established for the righteous, for the ones who keep the commandments of the Torah in this world. Indeed, "[t]he Torah is a tree of life to all who study it and those who keep its decrees will live. He will stand like a tree of life for the world that is to come. It is as good to study the Torah in this world as the fruit of the Tree of Life."[33] Paradise was thus linked to the covenant here and now, and also projected into the future, a collapsing of chronological time found again in *Targum Pseudo-Jonathan*: "Better is the Torah to one who observes it and walks in the paths of the way of life than the fruit of the tree of life; for the word of

---

30. Pss. Sol. 14.3–4; as quoted in ibid., 43.

31. Cf. ibid., 42.

32. Cf. ibid., 45.

33. Cf. ibid., 46.

the Lord prepared it for humanity to keep, that they would be established in the world to come."[34]

The projection of paradise into the future is the most obvious feature of apocalypses.[35] 1 Enoch 10.18–22 looks forward to the whole earth being tilled in righteousness, all planted with trees and full of blessing. Then later (1 En. 24–25) comes the vision of the seventh mountain, resembling the seat of a throne, with fragrant trees encircling it, and one tree with a fragrance beyond all fragrance, with leaves, blooms, and wood that would never wither, and beautiful fruit like the dates of a palm. The seer is told by the angel that the throne is God's, and after the judgment the fruit of this tree shall be available as food for the elect, those who are righteous and holy, and it will be transplanted to the holy place, the temple of the Lord. Similar pictures associating the tree with God's throne appear in 4 Ezra and the Life of Adam and Eve, where the tree produces healing oils, another motif found in Ephrem's association of paradise with the church and its sacraments; while the Testament of Levi 18.11 speaks of the holy ones eating from the tree of life. 4 Ezra 7.123, says that "Paradise, whose fruit endures incorruptible, wherein is delight and healing, shall be made manifest, but we cannot enter it because we have passed our lives in unseemly manners," though later at 8.52, we read:

> For, for you
> > is opened Paradise,
> > planted the tree of life;
> the future Age prepared,
> > plenteousness made ready;
> > a City builded,
> > a Rest appointed.

The association of these eschatological images is important for grasping the shifts in understanding that made the Eden story increasingly important in the period of early Christianity, where the book of Revelation picks up traditions of this kind:

---

34. As quoted in Anderson, *The Genesis of Perfection*, 180; Lanfer's translation on p. 48 of *Remembering Eden* is unclear.

35. Texts will be found among the *Apocrypha and Pseudepigapha*, ET R. H. Charles..

> Let anyone who has an ear listen to what the Spirit is saying to the churches. To everyone who conquers, I will give permission to eat from the tree of life that is in the paradise of God.
> (Rev 2:7)

> Then the angel showed me the river of the water of life bright as crystal, flowing from the throne of God and of the Lamb through the middle of the street of the city. On either side of the river is the tree of life, and its twelve kinds of fruit, producing its fruit each month; and the leaves of the tree are for the healing of the nations.
> (Rev 22:1–2)

This early Christian text subtly alerts us to another significant feature—the way the tree of life becomes something beyond the normal, something vast and cosmic: for how can it be at once on either side of the river? Lanfer provides many references to apocalyptic texts, Dead Sea Scrolls, and Targums depicting a cosmic tree of unimaginable size at the centre of the world, covering the whole earth. He adds: "The connection between the tree of life and the cosmic tree is made definitive in Christian interpretations of the cross of Christ as the representation of both."[36]

As we noted in chapter 1, Irenaeus speaks in the *Demonstration* of the cross as having cosmic dimensions, the Word of God invisibly pervading the whole creation—its length, breadth, height, and depth—so the Son of God was visibly crucified on a cross with those fourfold dimensions, inviting the dispersed from all sides, heights, depths, length, and breadth, to knowledge of the Father. In a Paschal homily attributed to Hippolytus,[37] the cosmic dimensions of cross and tree are made even more explicit:

> This tree of heavenly dimensions has raised itself from earth to heaven, fixing itself an eternal plant, between heaven and earth, to uphold the universe, support of all things, mainstay of the world, prop of the whole inhabited earth, joint of the terrestrial globe, holding together the variety of human nature, and nailed by the invisible bolts of the spirit, that being fixed to the divine, it may never more be sundered from it. Touching with its crown the summit of heaven, making firm the earth with its feet, and embracing on every side in its mighty arms the many spirits of the air between heaven and earth, it was wholly in all things and in every place.

36. Lanfer, *Remembering Eden*, 59.

37. Quoted in Daniélou, *Theology of Jewish Christianity*, 287.

Once the association of cross and tree of life was made, it is not difficult to see how all the motifs we have traced would come alive in the Christian imagination. As the tree of life was associated with the rivers rising in paradise to water the whole earth, so the waters of baptism received their power from the tree of life—the cross of Christ. In the sacraments of the church the fruit of the tree of life is eaten and healing oils administered: for Ephrem the revelation of the hidden tree of life on Golgotha permits his playing with these themes. The rich life of paradise is anticipated in the church through the cross of Christ, which brings eternal life. Further exploration of the church fathers would produce a wealth of allusions of this kind.[38] That the ancient Egyptian church adopted the Ankh (Fig. 2)—the hieroglyphic sign for life—as its form of the cross is hardly surprising.[39] For the Christian tradition, as well as its Jewish antecedents, the tree of life had become a multi-valent symbol, both sharpened and opened out by its identification with the cross.

FIGURE 2

Widening the Enquiry

However, the question now is whether further insights into construing the cross might come from widening the enquiry. This will take us outside my particular areas of expertise, but some preliminary investigation

38. See further, Murray, *Symbols of Church and Kingdom*, 114–29, 320–24; N.B. the symbolic associations with Vine and Olive.

39. Socrates, *Church History* V.17.

into the importance of the tree of life in other cultures, mythologies, and religions might possibly pay dividends. My own small collection of trees of life includes not only that little cross from l'Arche and a mosaic tablemat from the same workshop (Fig. 3), but also two floor rugs from Moslem countries, and photographs I took in Libya of the mosaic floor of an early Christian church (Figs. 4 and 5), which is a huge rendition of the tree of life remarkably similar to one of my small Moslem rugs (Fig. 6). These depictions almost invariably have birds lodging in the tree, as does a particularly striking representation of the Ankh in the Glazier Manuscript (Fig. 7). One is tempted to correlate these depictions of the tree of life with the parable of the mustard-seed (Matt 13:31–32),[40] a tiny seed producing a vast tree in which the birds of the air settle and make their nests; maybe, given that the parabolic tree represents the kingdom of God, it is meant to be conceived as a cosmic symbol like the tree of life. But the immediate point is the striking similarities of motif in different historical, cultural, and religious contexts.

FIGURE 3

40. I owe this observation to Kent Brower who raised the question when this lecture was delivered.

FIGURE 4

FIGURE 5

FIGURE 6

FIGURE 7

If you google "tree of life," you will find hundreds of images, old and new, and from many different cultures—even tattoos! The Wikipedia article begins with a smorgasbord of brief notes, under the heading "Religion and mythology," arranged neither chronologically nor logically, but in alphabetical order: Ancient Persia, Ancient Egypt, Armenia, Assyria (Fig. 8), Bahai faith, China, Christianity (with sub-heads on Mormons and Swedenborgians), Europe, Georgia, Germanic paganism and Norse mythology, Islam, Jewish sources (with a sub-head on Kabbalah), Meso-america, Middle East, North America, Serer religion, Turkic world. It then has a heading "Biology," which refers briefly to Darwin's famous doodle (Fig. 9), quotes from *The Origin of Species*, and illustrates subsequent uses of "tree of life" diagrams, not just to show the evolution of species, but also the microbiological relationships of bacteria and the most primitive life forms, archaea and eukaryota (Fig. 10). Further sections discuss the tree of life in contemporary art and architecture, music, literature, film, decorative arts— even video games. Is it possible to create a coherent account from all this? Does this symbol have the potential to integrate science, the creative arts, mythology, and religion? Or does Wikipedia's smorgasbord represent the fact that apparently common usage is purely coincidental?

FIGURE 8

FIGURE 9

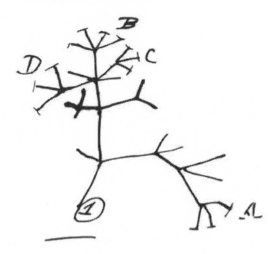

FIGURE 10

Phylogenetic Tree of Life

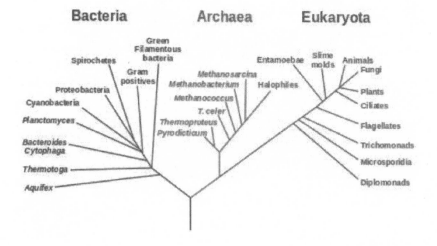

Maybe it is too ambitious to seek a unified account on quite such a grand scale, and yet I have come across one treatment of the Eden narrative that does attempt something like such a conceptual integration. *The Mythology of Eden* by Arthur and Elena George associates the motifs used in the Eden Narrative with the whole range of sacred trees in world mythologies:

> Connecting earth, heaven, and the underworld, and encompassing the traditional elements (earth, air, fire, and water), trees have represented life, renewal, rebirth, immortality, and unity in the cosmos, and have served as a connection with the divine above and below.[41]

They note that both of the two trees are in the midst of the garden, and therefore probably represent two aspects of the one sacred tree at the centre of the cosmos.[42] "As stylized trees, pillars and columns likewise symbolize the *axis mundi* and facilitate access to the divine, which explains why ancient temples featured columns/pillars so prominently in their architecture."[43]

Symbolically, they suggest, the World Tree is identical with Cosmic Mountain, and is the source of the waters of life.[44] Furthermore, the tree "embodied and symbolized divinity" and is most commonly associated the "Earth Goddess."[45] All these features are illustrated with examples from many different mythologies across the world, before the authors turn to the biblical world and its surrounding cultures.

Now the particular significance of the Asherah becomes clear. Earlier the authors had explained[46] that as a consequence of ancient and enduring mistranslations, only the advent of modern versions has revealed to the general reader some forty occurrences of Asherah in the Hebrew Bible, and only with the discovery of Ugarit in 1929 has it become possible even for Hebrew scholars to understand those biblical references. These Ugaritic texts make it clear that the god El and the goddess Asherah were the chief Canaanite divinities. A re-reading of biblical texts in the light of this material and other archaeological remains can reveal accommodation as well as resistance to Canaanite religion in Israel and Judah. Asherahs were a regular feature of high places—sacred poles, sometimes carved, which stood

41. George and George, *Mythology of Eden*, 140.

42. Ibid., 166.

43. Ibid., 141.

44. Ibid., 142–43.

45. Ibid., 144, 147.

46. Ibid., 69ff.

under sacred trees (Fig. 11).[47] To cite just three examples: Judges 3:7 reports that people served the Asherahs; 2 Kings 18:4 applauds the removal of high places along with their poles and columns, while 2 Kings 23:4ff. suggests it was necessary to destroy objects and symbols associated with the worship of Asherah in the temple itself. Many other references in the Bible reflect the prophetic attempts to uproot such worship, while indirectly providing evidence of its persistence. So George and George, following earlier scholars, speculate that Israel's God, Yahweh, was assimilated to the Canaanite god, El, and may have acquired El's wife in the process: hence the presence of Asherahs in Israelite places of worship, including the temple, against which the prophets protested. J's Eden narrative, it is suggested, deliberately subordinated the sacred trees to the one God, so contributing to the suppression of the motherly earth goddess, Asherah.

FIGURE 11

Like both Messinger and Lanfer, the authors of this global survey are cautious about tracing specific sources, acknowledging common motifs while drawing out the way in which biblical material offers critique of apparently similar myths. However, tracing what J was doing in his own context as distinct from subsequent interpretation of the story in terms of the fall and original sin, they have little sympathy for the way J, and indeed the wider biblical tradition, modified ancient mythological elements, so suppressing both the feminine and the desire for knowledge, while dealing with human potential for evil

47. A variety of examples of Asherahs are illustrated on Wikipedia.

through obedience to divine law. With Jungian psychological sympathy for mythology and symbolism, they endeavor to reclaim what lies behind the biblical text, and to appropriate its significance for our own understanding of the human condition. In the next chapter, we shall find reasons for being more receptive to the basic outlook of the Bible on obedience and disobedience. Now, however, the question for us is whether all this material might be used in a different way to help construe the cross.

A first point is immediately clear: this wider enquiry not only throws light on Genesis, but also on what apocalyptic texts and early Christianity made of Genesis—with its cosmic tree/cross reaching to all dimensions, sourcing the waters of life and bringing healing to the nations. To interpret the cross as the tree of life is to link it with a multicultural, if not universal, symbol of "life, renewal, rebirth, immortality, and unity in the cosmos," as well as serving "as a connection with the divine."[48]

A more daring suggestion would be that the cross as tree of life, with all its wider mythological associations, might evoke the nurturing and life-giving aspects of the ancient "earth mother," thus counterbalancing the patriarchal tendencies of the biblical material with the kind of gender ambivalences found in some medieval material. I think of Julian of Norwich[49] daring to speak of Christ's motherhood: "The human mother may put her child tenderly to her breast, but our tender Mother Jesus simply leads us into his blessed breast through his open side, and there gives us a glimpse of the Godhead and heavenly joy."[50] In this way Julian links the cross with the motherly love whereby the Son, the Second Person of the Trinity, made, sustained, and restored us. "When he made us God almighty was our kindly Father, and God all-wise our kindly Mother, and the Holy Spirit their love and goodness; all one God, one Lord."[51]

We might observe that this goes beyond the biblical suppression of the ancient "earth mother," rather taking up her power into the one Creator God through the generative role of the cross as tree. Christ becomes the maternal womb from whom we are born and through whom we are fed. "The human mother will suckle her child with her own milk, but our beloved Mother, Jesus, feeds us with himself, and, with the most tender courtesy, does it by means of the Blessed Sacrament, the precious food of

48. From above quote from ibid., 140.

49. *Julian of Norwich. Revelations of Divine Love*. ET Clifton Wolters.

50. Ibid., 60.

51. Ibid., 58.

all true life."[52] Thus the tree imagery becomes strangely aligned with the types of Passover and sacrifice through feeding us its life-giving properties.

Medieval Tree Imagery

We have turned to the Middle Ages to find ancient mythological associations potentially resurfacing, maybe unconsciously. And it is to the Middle Ages that we may look for further intriguing connections between the cross and the tree of life, again moving beyond my areas of expertise, but assisted by a much anticipated new publication which finally arrived in the post the very week I was working on the first draft of this chapter. Entitled *The Tree: Symbol, Allegory, and Mnemonic Device in Mediaeval Art and Thought*,[53] it is a collection of articles about the rich medieval development of tree symbols, bringing together in an interdisciplinary study images, diagrams, and texts to illuminate the multi-valence of the symbol, and reflecting an increasing volume of work devoted to this theme. Notable is the way tree diagrams or metaphors were used to organize knowledge and aid the memory. Ramon Llull (1232–316) produced an encyclopedic treatise, *Arbor scientiae* (*Tree of Knowledge/Science*), in which each of the sixteen chapters is arranged as a tree, in seven parts corresponding to the roots, the trunk, the branches, the twigs, the leaves, the flowers, and the fruit. Thereafter, according to Annamieke R. Verboon in an article on "The mediaeval Tree of Porphyry, an Organic Structure of Logic,"[54]

> The tree figure . . . was applied to various subjects: the Tree of Love, the Tree of Virtues, the Tree of Vices, the Tree of Science, the Tree of Life, the Tree of Knowledge, the Tree of Wisdom, the Genealogical Tree, the Tree of Jesse, the Tree of the Ten Commandments and the Ages of Man, the Tree of Affinity and Consanguinity, and the Tree of Heresies. . . . We can truly speak in terms of an inflation of tree imagery. How can we understand this tree mania in the 12th and 13th centuries?

The answer is found in the use of the tree image for preaching and instruction. "The sermon was supposed to be constructed like a tree, in which the introduction is like the trunk connecting the branches with the roots. . . .

52. Ibid., 60.

53. Edited by Pippa Salonius and Andrea Worm.

54. Salonius and Worm (eds.), *The Tree*, 95–116; quotation from pp. 107–8.

[T]he parts of the sermon are the branches on which the fruits of salvation, hang."[55]

Memory was understood to be "a consciously constructed system able to store and recollect different bits of information, like a library." A mental picture, such as a tree, could organize concepts, allowing instruction or meditation. Two of those listed trees are of particular interest to us.

FIGURE 12

The first is the Jesse tree[56] (Fig. 12) a particularly prominent iconographic form. Basically representing the genealogy of Jesus, variations on the theme are found widespread from the end of the eleventh century onwards, especially in stained glass. Its genesis is Isaiah 11:1: "There shall come forth a stem out of the root of Jesse, and a flower shall arise out of his root." Jesse usually appears lying asleep at the foot of the image, with the trunk of a tree emerging from him. Sitting on or enclosed by tree branches are several figures, usually kings such as David, with the Virgin Mary above and then, at the very top, Christ, often surrounded by seven doves representing the spirits of wisdom, understanding, counsel,

---

55. Salonius and Worm (eds.), *The Tree*, 108.

56. See Marie-Pierre Gelin, "*Stirps Jesse in capite ecclesiae*: Iconographic and Liturgical Readings of the Tree of Jesse in Stained-Glass Windows," in Salonius and Worm (eds.), *The Tree*, 13–33.

courage, knowledge, godliness, and fear of the Lord, referred to in Isaiah 11:2–3.

This presentation, however, is unlikely to be just about genealogy. It doubtless served in part to celebrate and exalt earthly kings—the figure of King Josiah in the window at Canterbury cathedral was apparently modeled on the great Seal of King Richard I from 1198. But the image also signifies the subjection of royal power to the church. Most versions show prophets alongside, emphasizing prophecy's fulfillment, types and antitypes, as well as the progression of history towards the last judgment—the figure of Christ at the top bearing similarities to his representation as final judge in great judgement scenes found so commonly in mediaeval cathedrals. Thus, the Jesse tree functioned as a synopsis of salvation history, evoking not only how Christ was foretold by the prophets, prefigured in kings, and destined to reign himself, but also the longstanding association of the tree with the cross, a correlation explicitly made in at least one version of the Jesse tree discussed in the book.

Besides this, the Jesse tree emphasizes the increasing significance of the Virgin Mary—in the Latin text of Isaiah *virga* is the word used for "stem"; through wordplay the virgin becomes the trunk and Christ the flower. Another beautiful medieval image reminds us how attention to the virgin could influence perception of the cross, namely the lily crucifix. (Fig. 13) The white lily represented purity and chastity, and in this image Christ hangs

FIGURE 13

in the petals of the lily flower, arms outstretched, as on the cross. It is as though Mary's virginity enfolds Christ's innocence, and turns the instrument of torture and death into something life-giving.[57]

Which brings us back to the tree of life, one of those tree themes that experienced substantial development in the Middle Ages. A treatise entitled *Lignum vitae* was written in about 1270 by the Franciscan scholar, Bonaventure.[58] In the prologue, he states that since imagination aids understanding, he has arranged his material in the form of an imaginary tree: in the lower branches the Savior's origin and life are described, in the middle his passion; and in the top his glorification. Each of these three main subjects is subdivided into four heads, constituting a total of twelve branches bearing twelve fruits. The tree of life bears twelve fruits, he explains, to correspond with the twelve fruits of the tree of life in Revelation 22:2, and there's a further allusion to this verse in the following sentence: "Imagine that the leaves are a most effective medicine to prevent and cure every kind of sickness, because the word of the cross is *the power of God for salvation to everyone who believes* (Rom. 1.6)."

This initial description also picks up paradise themes: the tree's roots are watered by an ever-flowing fountain that becomes a great and living river with four channels to water the garden of the entire church. Each fruit is then characterized by four incidents or aspects of the life, passion, or glorification of Jesus Christ.

Let me illustrate this from the section on the mystery of the passion:

- The fifth fruit is Jesus' confidence in trials; and it is substantiated by the betrayal, by Gethsemane, the arrival of the mob, and his arrest.

- The sixth fruit is patience in maltreatment, illustrated by Peter's denial, the blindfolding and abuse, the handing over to Pilate, and his condemnation.

- The seventh fruit is his constancy under torture, with outlines of the mockery, the nailing to the cross, the lifting up between two thieves, and his drinking of vinegar and gall as demonstrations.

- The eighth fruit is victory over death, captured by reference to the darkness and earthquake as he expires, his piercing with a lance, his dripping blood, and his burial.

57. The example in Fig. 13 is found in Long Melford Church, Suffolk, but similar images are apparently widespread dating from the period 1375–1500.

58. Available in English in Bonaventure, *The Soul's Journey into God, The Tree of Life, The Life of St. Francis*, ET Ewert Cousins.

Each characteristic with its supporting narratives is offered for meditation in a work meant to facilitate devotion and prayer.

Art works associated with this treatise are the subject of an article by Ulrike Ilg, "*Quasi Lignum Vitae*: The Tree of Life as an Image of Mendicant Identity."[59] For it was not long before the imaginative construct offered in this text was turned into "a didactic diagrammatic illustration," appearing in manuscripts, and then independently of Bonaventure's text—as, for example, a wall painting in a church, the frontispiece of a Bible manuscript, a panel painting for a Franciscan convent, a fresco for a Franciscan refectory (Fig. 14 depicts one example). In such visual representations cross or crucifix is superimposed on the diagrammatic tree, making clear the classic identification we have been exploring. The fruits issue from branches, which issue from the passion. The more elaborate depictions of the tree of life incorporate figures of the prophets, assimilating the tree of life design to the conventions of the tree of Jesse. The tree of life had again become a multi-valent symbol, like the tree of Jesse, encompassing salvation history. Both images put the cross at the centre, identifying it as the tree from which we may taste the fruit of eternal life.[60]

FIGURE 14

59. In Salonius and Worm (eds.), *The Tree*, 187–212.

60. See also Pippa Salonius, "*Arbor Jesse—Lignum Vitae*: The Tree of Jesse, the Tree of Life, and the Mendicants in Late Medieval Orvieto," in Salonius and Worm (eds.), *The Tree*, 213–41.

Concluding Reflections

So to my final reflections. There are again issues about the meaningfulness of the Eden narrative for twenty-first-century people, issues to which I will return in the final chapter. But, bypassing that for the moment, I briefly offer the following points.

1. On construing the cross as tree of life

As tree of life, the cross speaks of the superabundance of God's overflowing love for creation, becoming a sheer gift of grace. Paralleled with the tree of knowledge, the cross is associated with Adam's disobedience and its reversal; but associated with that other tree in the Eden narrative, the tree of life, the cross is turned into a source of healing and growth, offering the possibility of receiving and bearing fruits, becoming trees of righteousness, blossoming with the fruits of the Spirit. The cross can thus be construed as something about re-creation. If asked how this relates to theories of atonement my response would be that it transcends all of them, going beyond the rather enclosed frameworks of Anselm or the classic theory and, though closest to Abelard, going far beyond mere demonstration of God's love. It proclaims the blossoming and fruiting of God's gracious purposes through the tree of the cross.

2. On the coherence of creation and salvation

As tree of life, the cross surely helps to dissolve the long-standing tension in Christian theology between creation and atonement. It is the fruition of God's creative intentions, generating new life out of death. Incarnation and cross are turned into eschatological promise; and resurrection becomes integral to the cross, rather than its reversal or "happy ending." Besides, salvation is grounded within the existing created order, rather than implying transfer from one order to another—from a "gone-wrong" world to a "put-right" heaven. We are instead offered a process of transformative growth.

3. On the use of a universal symbol to construe the cross

As tree of life, the cross has a relationship to an apparently universal symbol in human culture across time and space, from mythology to science, from literature to film. Might this be developed imaginatively and creatively, I wonder, for the sake of mission and engagement with our post-modern cultural mix. The work on *The Mythology of Eden* might provide a cautionary note, suggesting as it does the appropriation of the mythological background rejected by the Scriptures. Yet there might be a hint towards a way forward in J's program of adopting and adapting motifs that have purchase in the surrounding culture, while also offering critique from a distinctive biblical perspective.

4. On the cross as an ecological sign

The tree of life symbol grounds the cross in the natural world, in the ecology of planet earth. Even without evoking mythological associations with Mother Nature, we may observe that trees benefit the earth and its creatures, sheltering birds, absorbing carbon dioxide, providing fruit for all kinds of animals, a source of health-giving medicines and drugs—offering leaves for the healing of the nations. If the cross is signified in trees, maybe it can be discerned anywhere: Ephrem observed that a bird cannot fly without stretching out its wings in a sign of the cross.[61] If we take seriously the notion that signs of the cross are to be found everywhere (a point to be pursued in the next chapter), then we may discern the reality that life was never meant to be cosy and comfortable, or insulated from pain and death, but rather, even in the midst of decay and dissolution, it is potentially joyous, creative, full of vitality, beautiful and variegated, a source of wonder and an earnest of transcendence.

---

61. Ephrem, *Faith* 18.6. Quoted by Brock in *The Luminous Eye*, 59.

4

Signs, Symbols, and Serpents

Signs, Symbols, Types

"Any study of non-literary Christianity must begin with signs and symbols," wrote Snyder at the start of his survey of archaeological evidence for Christianity before Constantine.[1] Narrative art, in the sense of pictorial representation of biblical stories, does not appear until after Constantine, and so there is no incontrovertible archaeological evidence for any pictorial or graphic depictions of the crucifixion at an early date, apart from, possibly, a teasing graffito found in 1856 in Rome in the servants' quarters of the Imperial palace on the Palatine hill. This caricatures a person raising his right-hand towards a donkey on a cross, and the rough lettering reads, when translated, "Alexamenos, worship god" (Figs. 15 and 16).

---

1. Snyder, *ANTE PACEM*, 23.

FIGURE 15

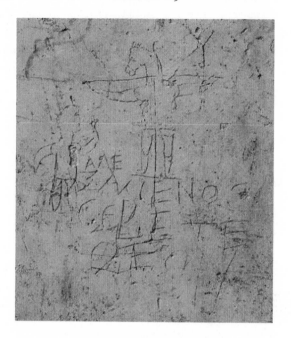

FIGURE 16

The date of this cartoon is hard to determine, but it does highlight the potential for mockery and misunderstanding, crucifixion signifying final defeat, disgrace, and shame. That has been advanced as an explanation for the absence of the cross in early Christian art; yet conversely, the very existence of this cartoon confirms that Christians were known to venerate a crucified man, and at the same time it makes even more telling the imaginative and creative ways in which Christians not merely came to terms with the death of Christ, but, with the aid of scriptural motifs, were able to re-mint it as signifying deliverance and life, as we have seen in earlier chapters.

In the absence of narrative pictures, then, what about signs and symbols of the cross? Last time we explored the cross as the tree of life, and found later art making the connection entirely explicit. The palm branch or palm tree was a widespread motif in ancient decorative art, almost certainly adopted by Christians as a sign of the tree of life. Often associated with the Good Shepherd in the catacombs and elsewhere (Fig. 17), such tree depictions probably point primarily to paradise;[2] but, as we saw last time, from a very early date, the tree of life already carried strong associations with the cross in early Christian texts. Was the palm motif a cryptic reference to the cross?

FIGURE 17

This opens up a distinctly controversial question among art historians. Though crosses figure as a widespread symbol in many ancient cultures, it

2. Ibid., 48.

is often noted that the earliest Christians did not apparently adopt the cross as such as a sign. They did adopt other signs, existing motifs from their contemporary culture which can only be identified as Christian when they appear with particular associations, or in particular locations, such as the catacombs. Classic examples of the use of such prototypes include images of Jonah, which borrow from depictions of Endymion, and the Good Shepherd, which copies the popular figure of a young man carrying a sheep (Fig. 18)—a long-standing and much used symbol of philanthropy.[3]

FIGURE 18

It is hard, then, to identify early Christian art forms, and even harder to be sure what interpretation the signs were given in their new context. Snyder identifies the following list of signs:

3. Jensen, *Understanding Early Christian Art*, 37.

1) lamb, 2) anchor, 3) vase, 4) dove, 5) boat, 6) olive branch, 7) the Orante, 8) palm, 9) bread, 10) the Good Shepherd, 11) fish, and 12) vine and grapes.[4]

The question is whether any of these represent the cross. The lamb, you would think, must surely signify what we were discussing in the first lecture—Christ as Passover; but no—in the earliest examples, according to Snyder, it appears with the Good Shepherd and probably signifies paradise; only later does the lamb come to be identified as the Lamb of God who takes away the sins of the world. What about the anchor (Fig. 19)? Snyder links this with boat and fish, suggesting it is a sign of security in the midst of persecution rather than a cryptic sign of the cross.

FIGURE 19

The Orante, a female figure with arms uplifted (Fig. 20), apparently represented filial piety on Roman coins and in funeral art; adopted by Christians and used in several contexts, it probably has similar familial associations, symbolizing the peace and prayer of the community, rather than Christ's arms stretched out on the cross.

4. Snyder, *ANTE PACEM*, 26.

FIGURE 20

Bread and fish (Fig. 21), vase, vine and grapes point towards the Christian *agape* meal rather than the eucharistic memorial of the passion; dove and olive evoke peace and deliverance. Snyder's survey concludes with the statement that "All the early symbols stress victory, peace and security in the face of adversity. . . . There is no place . . . for a crucified Christ, or a symbol of divine death. . . ."[5]

FIGURE 21

5. Ibid., 64.

Snyder is surely correct to insist that early on there is no representation of Christ crucified, nor any focus on the suffering and death of one believed to be Son of God. But the tendency to minimize signs of the cross in the early period is, in my view, properly contested by Robin Jensen in her book *Understanding Early Christian Art*.[6] Her argument is that, though over-interpretation in the past has encouraged caution, early Christian texts may appropriately be used to illuminate the matter. Some cross-markings on epitaphs in Rome and elsewhere can be dated to the third century, she says, while Tertullian indicates that the letter T was used as a sign on the forehead and comments that T is the very form of the cross, implying that this was predicted by Ezekiel 9:4–6.[7] The idea that the cross can be indicated by T is found as early as the *Epistle of Barnabas*, and by the third century Cyprian explicitly relates this sign to the passion and blood of Christ, referring to the Passover lamb fulfilled in Christ.[8] So other cryptic signs should perhaps not be so readily dismissed. It is noticeable how apologists suggested that signs of the cross were ubiquitous: e.g., Justin Martyr in his *I Apology* 55 suggests that the form of the cross is essential in the world: you cannot sail a ship without a cross-like mast; you cannot dig or do other physical work without tools that have a cross-shape; even the upright form of a human being, arms outstretched, shows the same cross-form. Trophies and banners, used as insignia of imperial power, display the shape of the cross. Somewhat later, Minucius Felix makes essentially the same points even more graphically:

> And, surely, your military ensigns, standards, and banners, what are they but gilded and decorated crosses? Your trophies of victory not merely copy the appearance of a simple cross but that of a man fastened to it as well. And as for the sign of the cross, there is no doubt that we see it in the world of nature around us: when you see a ship sailing with canvas swelling or gliding with oars extended; or when you set a yoke in place you form the sign of the cross; or when a man pays homage to God with purity of heart, stretching out his hands.[9]

Everything points to the cross, if only you have eyes to see. The Syrian poet Ephrem notes that unless a bird makes the sign of the cross it cannot fly:

6. Jensen, *Understanding Early Christian Art*, chapter 5.

7. Jensen in ibid. cites Tertullian, *Marc.* 3.22; and *Cor.* 3.

8. Jensen in ibid. cites *Ep. Barn.* 9.8 and Cyprian, *Demetr.* 22.

9. Minucius Felix, *Oct.* 29.6, as quoted by Jensen, ibid., 141.

> But if the bird gathers in its wings,
>
> thus denying the extended symbol of the Cross,
>
> then the air too will deny the bird:
>
> the air will not carry the bird
>
> unless its wings confess the Cross.[10]

These texts demand that we reconsider some of the signs listed earlier. Anchors and ships at least suggest the cross, and as for the Orante—if a person stretching out their arms in prayer signifies the cross, why not this figure? Tertullian specifically noted how the praying posture reflected the appearance of Christ on the cross: "taking our model from the Lord's passion, even in prayer we confess to Christ."[11]

And, if we move from such cryptic signs to scriptural types, then surely deeper meanings relating to the cross become ever more likely. The association of the lamb with the Good Shepherd in early Christian art is a case in point. In a text such as Cyprian's (noted above) the lamb and the T-sign are associated, and we need look no further than the New Testament for the Good Shepherd laying down his life (John 10:15), Christ, our paschal lamb being sacrificed (1 Cor 5:7), and "the lamb of God who takes away the sin of the world" (John 1:29)—a type well-developed in the earliest Christian literature, as we found in the first chapter. Jensen notes that Lactantius spoke of "the spotless white lamb itself as a figure of Christ: 'innocent, just, and holy; who, being slain . . . is the salvation of all who have written on their foreheads the sign of blood—that is, of the cross, on which he shed his blood.'"[12]

For Jensen another indirect representation of Christ's passion is the image of Abraham offering Isaac.[13] There are apparently two, possibly three, pre-Constantinian catacomb paintings of this theme, as well as sarcophagus reliefs; and more appear in the fourth century (Fig. 22).

10. Ephrem, *Faith* 18.6, as quoted by Sebastian Brock in *The Luminous Eye*, 59.

11. Tertullian, *Or.* 14, as quoted by Jensen, *Understanding Early Christian Art*, 36.

12. Jensen, *Understanding Early Christian Art*, 142.

13. See discussion in ibid., 143–48.

FIGURE 22

This narrative (discussed in chapter 2) is found as a type of Christ's sacrifice in many early Christian texts: the *Epistle of Barnabas*, Melito's *Peri Pascha*, Irenaeus, Tertullian, Clement, Origen, and the great later fathers, Ambrose, Ephrem, John Chrysostom, Paulinus of Nola, Gregory of Nyssa, Theodoret, and Augustine are listed by Jensen, who also notes liturgical use of the story in the Easter vigil. As noted in chapter 3, Isaac carrying the wood was associated with Christ carrying the cross: there we found Justin listing scriptural texts containing the word "wood" and associating them with the cross, including this example.

In the earliest texts two other "types" of the cross are frequent, neither, to my knowledge, reflected in the earliest Christian art, yet both deeply symbolic. The first is the figure of Moses, arms outstretched, while the Israelites fight Amalek (Exod 17:8–13). As long as Moses held his arms up, the people were victorious, but when they sagged, death overtook them. The *Epistle of Barnabas* 12 suggests this was to make them see that their salvation must depend upon putting their trust in him, and explicitly calls it a type of the cross and of him who was to suffer on it. Justin, *Dialogue* 90, takes up the same type, noting also that Jesus (Greek for Joshua) led the fight, and Moses prayed stretching out both hands, his arms supported by others so as not to droop when wearied. "For if he gave up any part of this sign, which was an imitation of the cross, the people were beaten . . . ; but if he remained in this form, Amalek was proportionately defeated, and he who prevailed, prevailed by the cross." Justin insists, then, that it wasn't just the fact that Moses prayed, but that he made the sign of the cross. Maybe the widespread use of this type reinforces the probability that the Orante (Fig. 20) signified the power of the cross.

Serpents

The second frequent type, often associated with the type just discussed, is the lifting up of the bronze serpent in the wilderness to counteract snakebite (Num 21:4–9); this too is found in the *Epistle of Barnabas* 12, in Justin *Dialogue* 91, and possibly alluded to in Irenaeus. But those employing this type were clearly puzzled by it. Irenaeus glosses over its potential problems, suggesting that even the law encouraged belief in the Son of God by saying "that human beings can be saved in no other way from the old wound of the serpent than by believing in him who, in the likeness of sinful flesh, is lifted up from the earth on the tree of martyrdom, and draws all things to himself, and vivifies the dead."[14] Irenaeus clearly recognized that John 3:14 alludes to the story in Numbers, and associates the snakebite with "the old wound of the serpent" in Eden, but he avoids direct association of the serpent with Christ.

The *Epistle of Barnabas*, however, does suggest that in the brazen serpent Moses made a symbol of Jesus, to show how he was ordained to suffer and give life to human beings. To convince the Israelites that the outcome of their sinning must be death,

> The Lord caused them to be fatally bitten by all manner of serpents—it having been through a serpent that sin first came into the world. So, even though Moses had personally given them the command, *you shall have no image, whether cast or carved, of your God*, yet now, to show them a symbol of Jesus, he constructed one himself. Moses made a serpent out of brass, set it up in a conspicuous position, and issued a proclamation . . . "whenever one of you is bitten, let him approach the serpent on the pole in a spirit of hope, believing that even though it is without life itself, it has nevertheless power to impart life; and he will recover at once."[15]

14. Irenaeus, *Haer.* IV.2.

15. *Ep. Barn.* 12.

Tertullian insists, like the *Epistle of Barnabas*, that the brazen serpent that the Lord commanded Moses to make was no pretext for idolatry, but was meant for the cure of those plagued by fiery serpents; he refuses to say what was figured by this cure.[16] You can sense both the potential attraction and the embarrassment of associating Jesus with a lifeless idol, especially in the form of a serpent. Justin is briefer and sharper:

> The spirit of prophecy by Moses did not teach us to believe in the serpent, since it shows us he was cursed by God from the beginning. The type or sign erected to counteract the serpents which bit Israel was intended for salvation for those who believe that death would be the serpent's fate through the one to be crucified, and that they, themselves, despite being bitten would find salvation by turning to the God who sent his Son into the world to be crucified.[17]

Justin is clearly worried by the possibility that the serpent would be associated with Jesus.

It is not hard to deduce why second-century Christians would find this type embarrassing, despite the authority of John's Gospel. Among the works of Tertullian[18] we find a statement to the effect that the gnostic sect of the Ophites magnify the serpent:

> to such a degree that they prefer him even to Christ himself; for it was he, they say, who gave us the origin of the knowledge of good and evil. His power and majesty (they say) Moses perceiving, set up the brazen serpent; and whoever gazed upon him obtained health. Christ himself (they say further) in his Gospel imitates Moses' serpent's sacred power in saying: And, as Moses lifted up the serpent in the desert, so it behoves the Son of Man to be lifted up. Him they introduce to bless the eucharistic elements.[19]

To identify Christ with the serpent was to be open to dangerous misunderstanding.

---

16. *Marc.* II.22.

17. *Dial.* 91.

18. Appended to Tertullian's *De Praescriptione Haereticorum* is a list and brief description of the heresies, which is now generally regarded as spurious. The veneration of the serpent by Ophites is attested elsewhere, but interestingly this particular statement explicitly appeals to the "type" under discussion.

19. *Praescr.* II.

This same ambivalence is reflected still in later allusions to this traditional type. Gregory of Nazianzus insists that the brazen serpent was hung up as a remedy for the biting serpents, not as a type of him who suffered for us, but as a *contrast*—it saved those who looked, not because they believed it to live, but because it was killed, and killed with it were the powers subject to it.[20] Conversely, Basil just accepts the tradition, listing the serpent on the standard among other types without comment;[21] and elsewhere using it as an example of what a sign is—by a sign, he says, understand in Scripture a cross.[22] Theodoret exploits the surprising idea that the brazen serpent is a type of the crucified Savior to justify other surprising comparisons.[23] Ambrose, however, explains it by linking it to another story about Moses:

> He cast down his rod and it became a serpent, which devoured the serpents of Egypt, thus signifying that the Word should become flesh to destroy the poison of the dread serpent by the forgiveness of sins. . . . The rod became a serpent; so he who was the Son of God, . . . lifted like the serpent on the cross, poured his healing medicine on the wounds of men. Wherefore the Lord himself says: "As Moses lifted up the serpent in the wilderness, so must the Son of Man be lifted up" (John 3:14).[24]

The power of the Serpent-Christ is at last acknowledged. My argument would be that following the patristic practice of interlinking different biblical texts, as Ambrose did, and taking the symbol further than any of the fathers anticipated, could lead us into one of the most intriguing and imaginative ways of construing the cross.

Recently I stepped into Ely Cathedral for the first time for many a long year, and was confronted with a vast artwork set against a plain wall—a snaking path leading up to a cross. Yes, the artist meant it to represent the way of life, but to me its sinuous form immediately suggested the Serpent-Christ, not least because this is a theme on which I have written and preached many a time. There is a real sense in which my journey with it lies at the heart of this project; so I need to revisit it, and hopefully re-present it rather than just repeat what has appeared in print before.[25]

20. *Orat.* 45.22.

21. *De Spir. S.* 31.

22. *Ep.* 260.8.

23. *Eranistes* III.

24. *Off.* III.15.94.

25. Notably in Young, *God's Presence.*

We shall start by going back to Eden and the contested narrative concerning the tree of knowledge. For most of Christian history, the fall of Adam and Eve has been the accepted interpretation. Time and again, the hapless couple have been depicted naked on either side of the tree of knowledge, its identification made clear, ever since the fourth-century sarcophagus of Junius Bassus (Fig. 23), by a serpent coiling around it, a motif repeated over and over in mediaeval cathedrals on reliefs, capitals, roof bosses, etc. Later, the snake is often shown as having a woman's head, her hands offering the tempting apple to Eve—for, of course, the seductive female serpent was really an embodiment of the devil.

FIGURE 23

But this reading of the Eden narrative did not always hold the field. Tertullian has already reminded us that early on there were those captivated by what Irenaeus called "knowledge falsely so-called," those now labeled "gnostics," and they apparently read this story upside-down—at least as mainstream Christian tradition has seen it. It was not, however, a reading entirely without justification.

To explore this further we must get under the skin of those gnostics. That is not an easy thing to do. Gnosticism is a subject I found alien as an undergraduate, avoided as a postgraduate, and subsequently taught as special final-year option; from which bit of personal history you will gather much about my ambivalence. Quite apart from the kaleidoscopic range of sects and texts, ideas and myths, not to mention potential sources—from biblical material to Greek philosophy and exotic Eastern religions, there are many puzzling aspects of Gnosticism. Bad enough is the apparent fragmentation of the divine, conceived in male-female pairs reproducing spiritual beings that populate the *plēroma*, the fullness of the spiritual world; but then there is the myth of *sophia*, which both alienates and attracts. In its Valentinian form, Sophia appears as one of thirty eternal beings that constitute the spiritual world, and, of course, her name means "wisdom." Sophia was filled with desire to know (an ambiguous word with both intellectual and sexual connotations); what she wanted to know was the ultimate *bythos* (a word meaning "depth" or "abyss")—the infinite, unknowable source of everything. As a result she conceived an "abortion" or "monstrous birth," a malformed child. Her issue was banished from the *plēroma*, and was known as Achamoth (a corruption of the Hebrew word for wisdom). It was Achamoth who gave rise to the Demiurge—the creator-craftsman who produced the material world in which now alien fragments of the spiritual world are trapped. The fall is conceived as pre-cosmic, and creation as the outcome of that disaster. It is by *gnōsis*—knowledge—that the spiritual ones, sparks of light from the spiritual world, are released to return to their true home from the tomb of the body (*sōma-sēma* is a Greek jingle expressing that notion that the body is a tomb). The knowledge required is esoteric, private, secret, only available to those in the know. Sometimes it is characterized as awareness of "who we are, where we came from, and where we're going to." It is, in other words, essentially knowledge of this gnostic myth that liberates the spirit from its alien environment. Sometimes this knowledge seems to be enshrined in magic passwords that enable the spirit to escape through the planetary spheres to the transcendent *plēroma*.

Now aspects of the implicit meaning are pretty transparent: gnostics believed they were an élite spiritual group trapped in an alien material environment, and the myth told them how that was so and offered *knowledge* as the way of salvation. Knowledge appears to be the prime value. But it is not common knowledge; nor is it philosophy in the sense of intellectual enquiry, however philosophical some of the terminology may appear (indeed, in Valentinianism the masculine-feminine pairs include key philosophical terms). Rather it is esoteric knowledge, a secret, a mystery known only by revelation, and therefore deeply anti-rational. The development of this myth clearly lies somewhere on the interface between Hebrew wisdom and Greek philosophy—an interface already clear in the books of Ecclesiastes,

Ben Sira, and the Wisdom of Solomon. It probably also has antecedents in apocalyptic. Not only is it clear that apocalyptic literature embraces wisdom elements, but gnostic and apocalyptic works have certain features in common. Both have strongly dualistic tendencies and both use highly symbolic and allegorical language. Furthermore, in apocalypses seers may be taken on space travel to see what the world looks like from heaven, so imparting knowledge about the geography of the universe, and some gnostic texts indulge in similar motifs. One might liken these fantasies to contemporary science fiction. Both bear some relationship to the real world and what human beings know about it, and yet weave this information into imaginative stories with many old motifs from folk-tales: conflict between goodies and baddies, quest for magic solutions, virtue tested and rewarded, and so on. Apocalyptic and gnostic texts alike display a sense of alienation from the world, yet draw deeply upon the culture they reject. The difference is that apocalyptic holds out hope that the one true God, Creator of everything, will in the end triumph over the opposing powers of evil, which seem to have the world in thrall, whereas gnostics are deeply alienated from the Creator God, dreaming of a spiritual world transcending this material creation in which they feel entrapped. Against this background it is easy to see how they could read the Genesis story as they did. The Demiurge or Creator-God forbids Adam and Eve to eat from the tree of knowledge in a bid to deny them the wisdom and knowledge that will allow their escape. The serpent is not the embodiment of the devil, but the embodiment of wisdom, with the word of salvation. Through the serpent, Adam and Eve receive *gnōsis* from the tree of knowledge.

That the serpent could represent wisdom in this way may seem at first sight surprising, but it really is not. After all, did not Jesus say, "Be wise as serpents" (Matt 10:16)? Snakes are both fascinating and fearful, and widely in the ancient world they were associated with wisdom, exceptional skills, and the power that comes with knowledge. The serpent was the sign of Asclepius, the Greek god of healing, and the Cretan goddess of wisdom was depicted with snakes in her hands. In the ancient Egyptian *Book of the Dead*, snakes appear in positive as well as negative guises—as hostile beings to be repulsed with spells, but also with magical powers for renewal of life. In the British Museum, at an exhibition entitled *The Ancient Egyptian Book of the Dead*, I saw a serpent-staff from about 1500 BC, an instrument enabling the holder to draw on the snake's supposed magical powers. Maybe this background context throws light on the strange stories to which earlier we saw Ambrose referring, apparently confusing the two versions. In Exodus 4, Moses is told to throw his staff on the ground and it turns into a snake, whereupon he runs away, but is told to catch it by its tail, and it immediately reverts to a staff. This was to be performed as a miracle to convince the Israelites that he should be believed and followed—it gave him the authority of one with exceptional knowledge and skill. Later, in chapter 7, Aaron is likewise told to throw down his staff and it turned into a snake. Then Pharaoh calls his wise men and by their magic they do the same, their staffs turning into snakes; but Aaron's snake swallows all the others. We are in a world in which wisdom and its magical powers are in contest. Serpents, both fascinating and fearful, were associated with such power, and the secret wisdom and knowledge by which it was exercised. It is hardly surprising that the members of one gnostic sect were called Naassenes or Ophites—clearly they were snake-worshippers (*Naas* = snake in Hebrew; *ophis* = snake in Greek), as Ps.-Tertullian implied in the passage cited above. The snake symbolized the knowledge or wisdom that brought them salvation.

An intriguing passage from Cyril of Alexandria's exegesis of the Pentateuch[26] shows how the complex associations of the serpent/staff imagery lived on and found new forms, not least through inter-textual associations. Commenting on the passage where Moses' staff converts to a serpent and then reverts to a staff, he develops the following allegory: the staff or scepter symbolizes kingship, for Adam was to rule the earth, but through the snake he was deprived of kingly glory, falling from paradise. The staff fell from the hand of Moses—this signifies that in the beginning there was in the hand of God a twig from paradise, made in God's image, in the glory of kingship, but he fell to the ground and in the eyes of God was like a snake. Moses fled from it; this is explained by quoting Wisdom of Solomon 1:5, "The Holy Spirit of wisdom will flee from deceit and back off from foolish thoughts," which shows how holiness and impurity, light and darkness, righteousness and unrighteousness are incompatible. Moses catches the snake by the tail, and that occasioned reversion into a scepter, a twig of paradise. So when God was pleased to recapitulate everything in Christ, creating anew what was made in the beginning, God sent us the Only Begotten, God's right-hand, the Creator and Savior of all. He took our humanity, transformed our wildness (i.e., the wild snake-form we had acquired), our sin, and through

26. Cyril of Alexandria, *On Worship in Spirit and in Truth*, Migne, *PG* 68.240–45; no ET available.

sanctification brought us back to royal honor and the tameness that leads to virtue.

All of this becomes the more telling if, once again, as in the case of the tree of life, the wider world of mythologies from across the globe is brought into play. A convenient conspectus is again provided by the book *The Mythology of Eden*,[27] and the ambivalence of the serpent, especially in the ancient Near East, becomes the more evident.

> Mythological symbols often have many meanings, but the serpent outdoes them all. A serpent can be portrayed as male or female, chthonic or celestial, lunar or solar; it can represent healing or poison, life or death, and it can assume related forms like dragons, sea monsters, hydras, and crocodiles.[28]

It has long been recognized that there are traces in the Hebrew Bible of creation-myths in which God overcame chaos by vanquishing a monster of the deep such as Leviathan; significantly, Genesis reduces such monsters to God's own creatures. But dragons and serpents continued to evoke the chaos that was conceived as constantly threatening to overwhelm the created order. At the same time, the serpent often *"represents the underlying divine cosmic energy, force, or power itself,* which is *one* and pervades the entire universe";[29] and again is often associated with the elemental Great Mother.[30] In Egypt the positive implications of the snake are articulated in upright depictions—indeed, the hieroglyphic sign for "goddess" is the upraised cobra; the negative associations are implied by showing it prone on the ground.[31] Serpents are not only linked with water, but are also frequently represented alongside trees. Archaeology has revealed the ubiquitous presence of serpent motifs across the biblical world, and in Canaan in particular, where serpents appear associated with the Asherah on plaques, scarabs, cult-stands and altars, jewellery and pottery.[32] In 2 Kings 18:4 we read that Hezekiah "removed the high places, broke down the pillars, and cut down the sacred pole [Heb. Asherah]. He broke in pieces the bronze serpent that Moses had made, for until those days the people of Israel had made offerings to it; it was called Nehushtan."

27. See previous chapter.

28. George and George, *The Mythology of Eden*, 177–78.

29. Ibid., 180.

30. Ibid., 183.

31. Ibid., 193–95.

32. Ibid., 197–201.

In the Eden narrative, then, J not only subordinated the sacred trees to Yahweh, but usurped the powers of healing and wisdom associated with the serpent. It was all part of the program of suppressing Canaanite religious symbols and practices, and ensuring that wisdom was found in obedience to the covenant with the one God. The serpent's punishment for tempting Eve was to go on its belly and eat dust (Gen 3:14); and so its negative connotations have prevailed in Christian culture.

Gnostics were neither the first nor the last to think it was a scandal that Adam and Eve should be denied knowledge. Wisdom is surely a good thing, as noted in modern times by many a biblical critic. It was obvious to gnostics that an alternative explanation should be sought, as indeed it had been for others too, according to Lanfer's reception history. Ben Sira 17 makes it clear that wisdom and understanding are divine gifts, while Philo associated paradise with wisdom, philosophy, and the contemplative life; the tree of life he considered "the knowledge, not only of things on the earth, but also of the eldest and highest cause of things."[33] In paradise, Philo thought, Adam was cultivating wisdom, but when driven out, he fell into ignorance. The value of knowledge is also admitted in the early Christian *Epistle to Diognetus* 12; speaking of the need to pass on what the Word impels us to utter "in our love for the truths revealed to us," the author continues:

> They [i.e., the revealed truths] become a very paradise of delight; they make a grove to spring up and flourish within themselves, which yields all manner of nourishment and adorns them with fruits of every kind. For in that garden are planted both the Tree of Knowledge and the Tree of Life—for it is not the Tree of Knowledge that causes death; the deadly thing is disobedience. Scripture clearly says, *In the beginning God planted in the midst of the garden the tree of knowledge and the tree of life*; thereby showing that the way to life lies through knowledge. It is only because the first created couple used it improperly that, through the wiles of the serpent, they were stripped of all they had. Without knowledge there can be no life, and without life there can be no trustworthy knowledge; which is why the two trees were planted side by side. . . . For a man who claims to know, but is without the knowledge which is real and attested by the life, knows nothing; the serpent has tricked him, because his heart is not set on life. But he who

33. See Lanfer, *Remembering Eden*, 75.

possesses knowledge coupled with fear, and whose quest for life is earnest, may plant in hope and look for fruit.

Knowledge and life seemed inseparable, and not just to gnostics; though they were the ones to follow the logic: the serpent lures Adam and Eve with the promise of wisdom, offering the gift of *gnōsis*, which enables the soul's escape. This beneficent embodiment of Sophia was the liberator to life worth having.

Now the idea that wisdom is the savior is also present in the New Testament. An explicit statement is found in 1 Corinthians 1:24: "Christ, the power of God and the wisdom of God." It is implied in Colossians 1:15–20, with its allusion to the creative role of personified wisdom described in Proverbs 8. That Proverbs text must also lie at the very heart of the first chapter of John, even though the word *sophia* is replaced by *logos* (= reason); and it is implied by the association of Christ with the healing and life-giving serpent in John 3:14, the type which the early church found so embarrassing: "just as Moses lifted up the serpent in the wilderness, so must the Son of man be lifted up." In Numbers 21:5–9 the antidote to snakebite is the bronze serpent lifted up on a pole, and that serpent becomes a type of Christ lifted up on the cross "that whoever believes in him may have eternal life."

The Serpent-Christ and the Cross

An odd coincidence led me to reflect on all this in a way I had never done before. Twenty-five years ago on a cycling holiday in France we stopped to look into an ancient, partly tumbledown church, and there was a modern crucifix, a very simple design—two differently shaded planes of wood, one in the shape of a cross, the other a curvaceous figure flattened against it. There for the first time I saw the Serpent-Christ. If you Google the Serpent-Christ, you will find a picture of a great modern representation of this theme located on Mount Nebo in Jordan (Fig. 24), the place from which Moses looked on the promised land he would never himself enter (Deut 34); but it is that French image, perhaps long since distorted in my memory, which stays with me (Fig. 25). A few days later I almost rode over a snake, basking in the sun on the roadside, beautiful, alluring, and a bit scary. The combination of those events was the trigger for meditation on a whole set of connections I had not made before, but crucial to understanding those biblical associations.

FIGURE 24

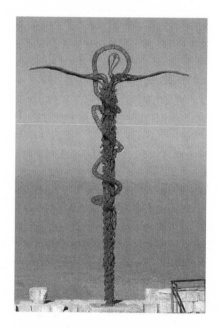

FIGURE 25

In 1 Corinthians 1–2 Paul sets up a contrast between worldly wisdom and the wisdom of God. According to worldly wisdom, the cross is foolishness, but the wisdom of the wise will be destroyed—Paul quotes Isaiah 29:14 to that effect. God has made foolish the wisdom of the world. Christ crucified is the power of God and the wisdom of God; for God's foolishness is wiser than human wisdom. Paul, like his converts, is not particularly wise by human standards, and his speech and proclamation were not with plausible words of wisdom—he decided to know nothing except Jesus Christ, and him crucified, so that their faith would rest, not on human wisdom, but on the power of God. He does speak wisdom among the mature, but it is not the wisdom of this aeon or of the rulers of this aeon. It is God's wisdom, secret and hidden, decreed before the aeons for our glory. The rulers of this aeon would not have crucified the Lord of glory if they had known, but to us this secret wisdom has been revealed. We discern it because we have the mind of Christ. Paul is sounding rather like the gnostics here, and we need to explore the biblical material further to discern the difference.

The contrast between human wisdom and divine wisdom is what John's Gospel hints at with the allusion to Numbers. The context of that story is the grumbling of the Israelites in the desert. Why on earth did Moses bring them out of Egypt to die in wilderness? There is no food or water; they detest this "miserable food," which is actually God's gift of manna. They are poisoned by commonsense, by the snakes of human wisdom. The antidote to this poison is the bronze serpent. So the antidote to the serpent in the Eden narrative is the Serpent-Christ: divine wisdom, rather than human wisdom.

A constant refrain in the biblical wisdom literature is that the beginning of wisdom is fear of the Lord. Yes, human skill and knowledge is celebrated, but true wisdom is hidden, known only to God (e.g., Job 28). Indeed, the ambiguities of human wisdom are tested in both Job and Ecclesiastes, and by the time we reach the wisdom books of the apocrypha (Ben Sira and the Wisdom of Solomon), obedience to the law and covenant becomes explicit as the key to wisdom. In the previous chapter we saw how it is this that makes the Eden narrative different from alleged parallels or supposed precursors. Obedience to God's word is given primacy. At the same time, however, a problem clearly lies in the human tendency to grasp at knowledge and wisdom, tempted by the serpent to be like God (Gen 3:4). In Ezekiel 28, often treated as drawing on an older form of the Adamic myth, the king of Tyre is described as having a proud heart, saying, "I am a god."

> Yet you are but a mortal, and no god,
>> though you compare your mind
> with the mind of God.
> You are indeed wiser than Daniel;
>> no secret is hidden from you;
> by your wisdom and your understanding
>> you have amassed wealth for yourself . . .
>> and your heart has become proud in your wealth.

Because of this *hybris*—the self-confident pride involved in comparing his mind with the mind of God—the oracle threatens his demise, and goes on to lament his fate:

> You were . . . full of wisdom
>> —perfect in beauty.
> You were in Eden, the garden of God . . .
> You were on the holy mountain of God . . .
> You were blameless in your ways
>> from the day you were created,
>> until iniquity was found in you.
> Your heart was proud because of your beauty;
>> you corrupted your wisdom
>> for the sake of your splendor . . .
> You have come to a dreadful end,
>> and shall be no more for ever.

Assuming that this characterization of the king of Tyre owes its language to a version of the Adamic myth, it is clearly closer than Genesis to ancient Near Eastern parallels in that the human being has wisdom to start with; however, that wisdom gets corrupted, leading him to overreach himself, and to claim godlikeness. Messinger[34] uses this to argue that the Eden narrative significantly shifts the focus of the older Adamic myth to highlight obedience and disobedience.

A key element in that act of disobedience is the human propensity to grasp or seize more than one has a right to. The serpent tempts Eve with the promise of being like God, and grasping is highlighted alongside disobedience in the contrasting depiction of the figure of Christ as true wisdom found in Philippians 2: he did not think equality with God a thing to be

34. Cf. discussion in the last chapter.

grasped, but rather emptied himself and was *obedient* unto death, even death on the cross (Phil 2:6–8). Indeed, for me, F. C. Burkitt, in his book *Church and Gnosis,*[35] long since offered a significant clue to the real import of the gnostic myth of Sophia. The myth is about the tragedy of Sophia, a figure representing the failure of human wisdom and knowledge. In Greek tragedy the *nemesis,* the retribution or fate that comes upon the great hero, often arises out of *hybris:* frequently translated "pride," the word connotes a kind of over-reaching of oneself, an attempt to be more than human, an outrageous challenge to the gods (cf. Ezekiel 28 above)—not so much a weakness in character, as the inevitable obverse of the hero's greatness. So the significance of the myth of Sophia was precisely the fall of wisdom, the failure of human understanding, the *hybris* of the attempt to know, ambition over-reaching itself, the impossibility of human attainment to knowledge of the ultimate, the sin of that desire to know the *bythos,* the infinite depth of the divine. Wisdom driven by desire for attainment—intellectual mastery, we might say, was ultimately corrupted. You could only get wisdom and understanding by receiving it through revelation.

So how does Paul differ from the gnostics? He too speaks of hidden knowledge and divine wisdom revealed. But whereas the gnostics projected Sophia's *hybris,* her grasping at knowledge of the divine, onto the heavens, Paul locates the struggle within humanity: "the good that I would, that I do not, and the evil I would not, that I do" (Rom 7:19). The gnostics turned the fall into a pre-cosmic explanation of how spiritual beings got trapped in the material world; Paul points to the fundamental disobedience that has corrupted human wisdom (cf. Rom 5:14ff and 1 Cor 1:18ff; 2:8). For Christian gnostics there was a lineage of revealers, beginning with the serpent, going on through Seth, and including Christ, but a spiritual rather than a crucified Christ for whom it was not necessary to die; for Paul and his successors, martyrdom is the ultimate testament to loyalty and obedience to the Christ who was obedient unto death. The gnostics offered liberating knowledge that imparts transcendence despite exclusion from the *plēroma,* turning this life into a transient illusion; whereas Paul offers an antidote to sin's poison, the *plēroma* of God's wisdom embodied in Christ, in whom we may become a new creation. The Gospel of John captures this in that allusion to Numbers: "just as Moses lifted up the serpent in the wilderness, so must the Son of man being lifted up, that whoever believes in him may have eternal life."

35. Published in 1932.

Concluding Reflections

1. Signs of God's healing activity rather than atonement

The intricate associations of the serpent-sign suggest healing—an antidote for poison; in other words, humankind is not itself entirely responsible for the human condition—"the good that I would that I do not" (Rom 7:19). Other signs tend to signify predominantly protection or victory. Consistently, then, the signs of the cross used in the early church represent God's action to put things right, rather than some kind of atonement offered to God or attempt to satisfy God's demands. Atonement theories seem wide of the mark, apart from Aulen's "classic theory," which was certainly the predominant patristic approach. It is interesting that one expression of that "classic" viewpoint creatively brought together Scripture and the associations of serpents and dragons found in those underlying ancient myths:

> He is called Worm because he said, "I am a worm and not a man" [Ps 22:6]. By the brightness of the Godhead, as a hook in a worm, thus he hid his own Godhead in his body and cast it into the nether regions of the world and drew it up like a good fisherman; about whom he says, "He took the dragon with a hook and put a bridle in his mouth and a spike through his nose" [Job 41:1-2], that is the devil he took and whose wiles he broke, about whom the Psalmist David bears witness, "Thou has broken the heads of the dragon" [Ps 74:13].[36]

The idea expressed here is found earlier in Gregory of Nyssa:[37] that the devil was offered Christ as a ransom to free humanity from death; he accepted it, but was deceived into trying to gulp down the deity with the bait of flesh and could not hold onto the principle of life and light. Often dismissed as crude and morally suspect, this image is perhaps more comprehensible if set against the mythological symbols explored in this chapter. Thus interpreted, victory over the negatively viewed serpent construes the cross as God's powerful triumph over sin and the powers of evil that lurk behind it. However, the motifs of healing, protection, and life associated with the positively viewed serpent may provide gentler ways of seeing it. The point is that God is understood, not as the recipient of an atoning ransom or

36. Quoted from the translation of a sermonic address in *The Martyrdom of St Abo of Tiflis,* found in Birdsall, "Diatessaric Readings in the Martyrdom of St Abo of Tiflis," 313-24.

37. *The Great Catechism,* 24.

placatory offering, but as the compassionate initiator and merciful executor of human salvation.

2. Wisdom and the human condition

We focused earlier on obedience and disobedience, and on God's merciful recapitulation in Christ. It is worth recalling also the patristic insight that God's banishment of Adam was an act of mercy that allowed for the possibility of restoration (see chapter 3). All this suggests the ambiguity of the human condition rather than the kind of catastrophic fall associated with Western Christian theology since Augustine. The ambiguity of wisdom reflects this, suggesting that human cleverness tends to become corrupted[38] by desire for ever more power, while true wisdom recognizes that wisdom and understanding are divine gifts, and involve a certain humility and "fear of the Lord." Autonomous human wisdom makes claims conflicting with the reality of our creatureliness, and countercultural though it be, a challenge needs to be offered to modernity's critique of obedience to divine law.[39] The perspective of the fathers on the immaturity of Adam and Eve has been reclaimed in some modern reflections on the story;[40] children need structures and discipline. And not just children: modern assertions of human autonomy conflict with the perception that human flourishing requires moral frameworks and human society cannot function without the structures of law. Absolute freedom is an illusion. Wisdom requires self-knowledge, the recognition that human individuals are part of a larger whole, while humankind as a whole is part of a larger created order, which human presumption is in danger of harming. We need to re-appropriate the significance of obedience and "fear of the Lord." As the Wesleyan tradition has always insisted, the law cannot save, for we are saved only by grace through faith, but saving grace enables works of the law.

---

38. The classic Latin tag is *corruptio optimi pessima*—the worst thing is the corruption of what is best.

39. See previous chapter.

40. E.g., Hick, *Evil and the Love of God.*

3. Towards a more universal perspective

I have offered a hint that the tragedy of Sophia's fall, and indeed of the fall of humankind represented in Adam and Eve, parallels the reality of *hybris* and *nemesis* in tragic literature. This insight was touched on in chapter 2 and will be followed up further in our final chapter. Along with the parallels found in worldwide mythologies, it helps to depict the cross on a wider canvas than Christian theological traditions, linking it with insights concerning the human condition found in significant cultural forms in other traditions.

4. Perceiving the cross in our everyday world

Going back to our initial exploration of the manifold signs and symbols of the cross, could this carry any significance for us? Well, the tree of life could lend itself, perhaps, to the symbolism of blossom, fruit, and health-giving leaves, pointing to paradise and eschatological promise, as we saw in the last chapter; but are any others at all promising for our own reflection, especially when it is a case of simply correlating miscellaneous things with the shape of the cross? I have two potentially creative observations to make:

(i) The plethora of signs in nature and everyday life might encourage us to perceive the cross everywhere, in all kinds of unlikely places, so enriching meditation. I once came across a little book called *Long Wandering Prayer*,[41] which encourages going on long solo walks and allowing everything you see or meet, even your own wandering thoughts, to become worship, thanksgiving, or intercession. Cross-shapes, like those discerned by the fathers, might meet us at every turn if we have eyes to see, and they could then focus thoughts and prayers.

(ii) The sign of the cross in our world might be the suffering of innocents, the abuse and atrocities we are constantly confronted with in the news and to which our culture is now so sensitive. This has produced already an approach to the cross that goes beyond anything in the tradition: the cross is now widely treated as a sign of God so loving the world that in Jesus Christ God's very self identified with, indeed entered into, that surd of suffering that seems to challenge God's goodness and the goodness of the divine creation,[42] God thus taking responsibility for it all and suffering

41. Hansen, *Long Wandering Prayer: An Invitation to Walk with God.*
42. E.g., Moltmann, *The Crucified God*; Fiddes, *The Creative Suffering of God.*

alongside. In this perspective the cross reinforces the saying of Jesus, "Not a sparrow falls without your heavenly Father." This is an insight into the cross that was simply not possible for the patristic era, but one that might follow for us from their perception of signs pointing to the reality of the cross in all kinds of patterns and places in the life of humankind on earth.

5

Language, Liturgy, and Life

The time has come to review various issues arising from the examples we have considered—indeed, to return to discussion of methodology and its theological basis. We have visited worlds that may seem strange, emphases that may not seem to impinge on us easily, for all kinds of reasons. We are likely to have questions about language, factuality, historicity, and truth—questions that arise from modernity. Even though post-modernity has enabled a plurality of free-floating ideas and visionary associations to have a bit more scope, we still tend to be suspicious of allegory, let alone myth, while symbolism and metaphor we want translated, and we prefer theoretical exploration to intuitive insight. Yet I have suggested a move from theory to *theōria*, to a kind of spiritual discernment that comes through imaginative engagement with Scripture rather than literalizing exegesis. I have illustrated this with examples from earlier Christian periods and tentatively suggested they might in some measure be reclaimed.

But questions remain. How relevant to us are these insights? How might we find insights more obviously inspiring for our own time? Hopefully some answers will emerge as we take up issues suggested by what we have been observing and relate them to broader questions in theological studies, drawing on some aspects of my previous work.[1] To provoke reflection as we go along. I shall punctuate this chapter with five cruciform poems whose composition was inspired by working on this project. Here is the first:

1. E.g., in particular, Young, *God's Presence.*

Tree of life

Fruiting from that?
That gnarled
broken bole
old
partially rotting
but vertical
still
hollow, concave—a cleft in which to hide
open as if an inviting embrace, but dead
surely dead as a dodo just lifeless wood
protruding
outstretched
branches
a bouquet
of thorns
twisting boughs
contorted
knotted joints
darkly
silhouetted
against the sun.
But pass behind and
a miracle is revealed
bathed in light
from the golden afternoon sky
twiglets branching forth
from the brittle bark
fresh green leaves
healing and softly alive
buds promising blossom and fruit profuse:
fruiting from that?—of course, the true vine
the tree of life, rooted in paradise

Theological Language

Clearly the nature of theological language is an issue that lies at the heart of this enterprise. I believe we have more to learn from early Christian thinkers than from most of the twentieth-century philosophical discussions of religious language. Rowan Williams' recent Gifford lectures, *The Edge of Words*, engages in a discussion more sophisticated than most, both with current philosophy and with the science of language; his position strikes me as somewhat similar to the fathers when it comes to exploring ways in which we speak of God. So I suggest we begin by considering how Ephrem, the Syrian poet of the fourth century, justified his use of poetry as a theological medium.

Fundamentally, Ephrem's theology was grounded in the impossibility of reducing God to the limits of human language. In the face of heretical claims about the definition of what is truly divine, he, along with others in the period, asserted that to define is to set limits or boundaries on God, and so is basically blasphemous. Indeed,

> Whoever is capable of investigating
> > becomes the container of what he investigates;
> and knowledge which is capable of containing the omniscient
> > is greater than Him,
> for it has proved capable of measuring the whole of Him.
> A person who investigates the Father and Son
> > is thus greater than them!
> Far be it, then, and something anathema,
> > that the Father and Son should be investigated,
> while dust and ashes exalts itself![2]

God is hidden. Yet God has revealed the divine self. Brock identifies three ways of divine self-revelation in Ephrem's work. In addition to the incarnation there is the presence of types and symbols in both nature and Scripture, and then there are the "names" or metaphors that God allows to be used of the divine self in the Scriptures. The types and symbols are pointers—to us they may seem to be revelatory of some aspect of the divine, but from God's perspective "some aspect of the divine reality lies hidden in the type or symbol."[3] In other words, the pointers both reveal and conceal—you cannot

2. Ephrem, *Faith* 9.16, as quoted by Sebastian Brock in *The Luminous Eye*, 13.

3. Brock, *The Luminous Eye*, 26–27.

take them literally, yet neither can you divorce symbol from reality. The Syriac word Ephrem uses for "symbol" is one that includes the meanings "secret" and "mystery," and this "mystery" carries the hidden power that lies behind it. Thus, creation and Scripture are full of signs that speak to us of God, but always obliquely; we get glimpses of the hidden reality. In Scripture, however, we get more than these types and symbols; for God has clothed the divine self in human language. Ephrem speaks time and again of God putting on "names." Mostly they are metaphors drawn from our human experience—and Ephrem understands this as an act of immense condescension. I shall quote him at some length here:

> Let us give thanks to God, who clothed Himself in the
> names of the body's various parts:
> Scripture refers to His "ears," to teach us that He listens
>   to us;
> it speaks of His "eyes," to show that He sees us.
> It was just the names of such things that He put on,
> and, although in His true Being there is not wrath or
>   regret,
> yet He put on these names too because of our weakness.

> Refrain; Blessed be He who has appeared to our human
> race under so many metaphors.

> We should realize that, had He not put on the names
> of such things, it would not have been possible for Him
> to speak with us humans. By means of what belongs
>   to us did He draw close to us:
> He clothed Himself in our language, so that He might
>   clothe us
> in His mode of life. He asked for our form and put
>   this on,
> and then, as a father with His children, He spoke with
> our childish state.

> It is our metaphors that He put on—though He did
>   not literally do so;
> He then took them off—without actually doing so:

when wearing them,
He was at the same time stripped of them.
He puts one on when it is beneficial, then strips it off
    in exchange for another;
the fact that He strips off and puts on all sorts of
    metaphors
tells us that the metaphor does not apply to His true
    Being:
because that Being is hidden, He has depicted it by
    means of what is visible . . .

A person who is teaching a parrot to speak
hides behind a mirror and teaches it in this way:
when the bird turns in the direction of the voice which
    is speaking
it finds in front of its eyes its own resemblance reflected;
it imagines that it is another parrot, conversing
    with itself.
The man puts the bird's image in front of it, so that
    thereby it might
learn how to speak.
This bird is a fellow creature with the man,
but although this relationship exists, the man beguiles
    and teaches
the parrot something alien to itself by means of itself;
    in this way he speaks with it.
The Divine Being that in all things is exalted above all
    things
in His love bent down from on high and acquired from
    us our own habits:
He laboured by every means so as to turn all to Himself.[4]

The danger is that the use of these names can lead us to drag God down to our level when they were intended to drag us upwards.

---

4. *Faith* 31; as quoted in Brock, *The Luminous Eye*, 60–62.

God has made small His majesty
> by means of these borrowed names.
For we should not imagine
> that He has completely disclosed his majesty:
this is not what His majesty actually is,
but it represents only what we are capable of:
what we perceive as His majesty is but a tiny part,
for He has shown us a single spark from it:
He has accorded to us only what our eyes can take
of the multitude of His powerful rays.[5]

If someone concentrates his attention
solely on the metaphors used of God's majesty,
he abuses and misrepresents that majesty
by means of those metaphors
with which God has clothed Himself for man's own benefit,
and he is ungrateful to that Grace
which has bent down its stature to the level of man's childishness;
even though God has nothing in common with it,
He clothed Himself in the likeness man
in order to bring man to the likeness of Himself.[6]

Ephrem understands Scripture as a fountain. No reader ever exhausts it. Each should give thanks for what they've taken from it, and neither complain about what is left over, nor fail to recognize that what is left behind can still be their inheritance.[7]

The Cappadocian Fathers, Gregory of Nazianzus and Gregory of Nyssa, are likewise clear that human language is inadequate for articulating God's reality.[8] Nazianzen insists that God is known not in essence, but in activities:

> The divine cannot be named. . . . For no one has ever breathed the
> whole air, nor has any mind located, or language contained, the
> Being of God completely. But sketching God's inward self from

5. *Heresies* 30.4; as quoted by Brock, *The Luminous Eye*, 65.

6. *Paradise* 11.6; as quoted by Brock, *The Luminous Eye*, 47–48.

7. *Commentary on the Diatessaron* 1.18–19; quoted by Brock, *The Luminous Eye*, 50–51.

8. See further my discussion in Young, *God's Presence*, ch. 8.

outward characteristics, we may assemble an inadequate, weak, and partial picture. And the one who makes the best theologian is not the one who knows the whole truth . . . [b]ut the one who creates the best picture, who assembles more of truth's image or shadow.[9]

A multiplicity of scriptural "names" is necessary to capture this outline.

Nyssen develops this further, grounding his theory of religious language in a general theory of language. The existence of different languages indicates that God gave freedom to humankind to invent linguistic expression. So, "whereas no one suitable word has been found to express the divine nature, we address God by many names, each by some distinctive touch adding something fresh to our notions of him."[10] However, "we do not say that the nature of things was a human invention, but only their names"; and the names we use of God are more than a figment of the human imagination: creation and Scripture are expressive of God's will and truth since God cannot be a party to deception. God accommodates the divine self to the limitations of human language and conceptuality. Gregory's classic example concerns the Son of God: in the case of divine sonship, the mind has to exclude sex and passion, even a specific act in time; so sonship as we know it cannot be what it is about; yet that does not mean it is meaningless—we have to think simply of the Son as being eternally derived from the Father. This kind of thing applies to every term used, so the only way to get an idea of God at all is to multiply names, attributes, and images, one counterbalancing another: "because . . . there is no appropriate term to be found to mark the subject adequately, we are compelled by many and differing names . . . to divulge our surmises . . . with regard to the deity."

Furthermore, though you may begin with the most obvious and natural sense of each name, you have to recognize that with reference to God they are used with a heightened and more glorious meaning. Gregory is clear that theological language has a basis in God's self-revelation, even though every term used is transcended by the divine reality, and that paradox, the counterbalancing of one notion with another—even its opposite—can alone ensure that that language is safeguarded from the blasphemy of a crude literalism.

9. *Orat.* 30.

10. The source of Gregory's discussion and my quotations is *Contra Eunomium*, especially Book I (Jaeger's enumeration; Book II in *NPNF* translation).

Like Gregory, Rowan Williams grounds his account of how we speak about God in a general theory of language: language is always symbolic in that it represents reality in another medium. Representation is the key concept: language inevitably consists of symbols—even everyday language is far from what people think they mean by literal. Language, like art or music, is plastic and creative, generative of competing expressions and incompleteness. It is also embodied—indeed Williams' argument leads to the assertion that matter is itself inescapably symbolic, and so through symbols the created order can be redolent of God:

> [E]very finite phenomenon is at some level a carrier of divine significance; it is a symbol, . . . something indicating God or carrying meanings fully or adequately intelligible only when unconditioned intelligence is assumed. One can take this as a licence for an approach to the world which looks everywhere for allegories of the divine, ciphers to be decoded[;] . . . there is in every situation the possibility for the human intelligence to receive some kind of formation by the infinite intelligent act of God. Our skills in discernment and interpretation—the skills associated with the gift of prophecy . . .—are activated so as to produce new levels of understanding of our calling . . . [;] each situation is a "word" from God.[11]

Like the fathers, Williams regards this as an extension of our everyday use of language in which paradox is an essential way of triggering "a process of reshuffling the conceptual pack," and "'extreme' forms of utterance" are a way of enlarging "our notion of what it is to produce a 'truthful' way of speaking about what is in front of us."[12] So language is bound to seem "eccentric," and "the 'crudest' metaphors for God are often the most successful, just because no-one could mistake them for accurate descriptions."[13] Williams first notes God as Rock, or Fire, then adduces Jesus' use of parables—the representation of God by a "whole narrative," sometimes "carefully calculated shocks," like the Unjust Steward or the Unjust Judge. The embarrassment of extreme or inappropriate analogies provokes us into new perceptions and weans us off the inadequacies of literalism.

Now it seems to me that this approach to theological language is vital when it comes to construing the cross. No one theory of atonement

11. Williams, *The Edge of Words*, 120–21.

12. Ibid., 128.

13. Ibid., 148–49.

is adequate—each carries elements inappropriate to the situation because they are projections of human assumptions about justice, mercy, love, propitiation, expiation, forgiveness, victory, liberation, etc., etc. To suggest that God has to exact a penalty for sin is blasphemously to subject God to a principle outside the divine self. To suggest that the Son has to placate the wrath of the Father is to drive a coach and horses through the doctrine of the Trinity, itself a concept of God that requires subtle counterbalancing of opposing ideas. Put in such terms these statements are, of course, caricatures—"extremes," to use Williams' way of putting it—and in each atonement theory there are vital insights to be found, as I have shown in previous work.[14] All I want to suggest now is that no single one contains the whole truth and nothing but the truth. To imagine that it might is not simply to set limits on potentially explosive meaning, but to claim control over it. Furthermore, it seems to me significant that the fathers never came up with a single theory—rather they drew on a multiplicity of images and associations, signs and symbols, of which we have explored just a few in earlier chapters. We need to embrace Rowan Williams' insight that "When we think with images, either in art or religion, we are genuinely thinking."[15]

So let me insert my second poem, *Paradox*. It juxtaposes the historical particularity of the cross with the patristic sense of it as cosmic and eternal, sharpening up for us the way it is, paradoxically, both universal and unique.

14. E.g., Young, *Can These Dry Bones Live?*; Young, *God's Presence*, et al.
15. Williams, *The Edge of Words*, 194.

Paradox

Infinite

its reach

its feet

on the ground

its arms outstretched embracing cosmic space

constricted though they be by wood and nails

pointing beyond yet printing its shape just here

always

positioned

in one

particular

place

a single

moment

in time

one victim's

pain

which somehow

exposes

all creation's hurt

it showers

blood, sweat

and tears

cleansing

cascades

restoring

vitality

its feet touch earth

its reach is infinite

Myth and History

The historical particularity of the crucifixion is held in tension with its universal significance. This necessitates consideration of the old much-discussed issue of myth and history, as do certain persistent features of the signs, types, and symbols we have been exploring: many of the previous chapters have drawn on the opening chapters of Genesis, aspects of the story of Adam and Eve, visions of paradise, both primordial and eschatological. I hardly need spell out the difficulties that our culture has with such a focus. The theory of evolution not only challenges the biblical account of creation, but also inevitably reduces the Eden narrative to myth. That myth can illuminate the human condition was the assumption of the book *The Mythology of Eden*, to which a good deal of reference has been made. Yet how can we take seriously the typological parallel between Adam and Christ when one character belongs to myth and the other to history? Surely there is a danger of reducing the gospel to myth in the process.[16]

Once again, the poetry of Ephrem can give us a lead. Let me quote select stanzas from the 13th *Hymn on Paradise*:

> The king of Babylon resembled
> Adam king of the universe:
> both rose up against the one Lord
> and were brought low;
> He made them outlaws,
> casting them afar.
> Who can fail to weep,
> seeing that these freeborn kings
> preferred slavery
> and servitude.
> Blessed is He who released us
> so that His image might no longer be in bondage.

Ephrem goes on to suggest that God depicted Adam in king David, who "provoked God by his exercise of kingship," and "God stripped him of that kingship";

> and only when he repented did he return.
> to his former abode and kingship.

16. See further, Young, *God's Presence*, ch. 5.

Blessed is He who has thus taught us to repent.
    so that we too may return to paradise.

Because it was not easy
    for us to see our fallen state—
how and whence we had fallen
    at the very outset—
He depicted it all together
    in that king,
portraying in our fall
    his fall,
and portraying our return
    in his repentant return.
Praise to Him who delineated
    this likeness for the repentant . . . .

Samson had to grind up the mill,
    Adam had to labour wearily on the soil;
Samson prayed
    to be released,
whereas we pray,
    to grow old in our misery.
Blessed is He who delivered Samson,
    releasing him from the grinding.

Samson is a type of the death
    of Christ, the High Priest:
Samson's death returns prisoners
    to their towns,
whereas the High Priest's death
    has returned us to our heritage.
Let us repeat to each other
    the good news in joy,
that the gate is once again open,
    and happy is he who enters in quickly.
Blessed is He who has not made us
    outlaws never to return.

Observe what is happening here. Adam is clearly a representative or universal figure, one who lives in "everyman." That indeed is what his Hebrew name implies. In intriguing ways, the Christ of the New Testament, as well as being a particular historical person, is a parallel representative or universal figure. It is not just that in Christ we all become a new creation, adopted sons of God, conformed to his likeness, but that the drama of the gospel narrative exposes recurring aspects of the human condition, the deep "flaw" in human being. The hero of the story, presented to us as one who, as an innocent prophet, challenged the vested interests and uneasy *status quo* of his time, is judicially disposed of by the structures and powers of the day. People flock after him, then turn against him. He is roughed up by soldiers guarding him, and the authorities wash their hands of responsibility. He is progressively isolated—the disciples sleep in the garden, the betraying friend kisses him, the right-hand man denies him, the crowds desert him, and finally he cries out, "My God, my God, why hast thou forsaken me?" As Girard put it (cf. chapter 2), the death of Jesus is banal—or rather, it is a paradigm story, exposing human reality. With memories haunted by Holocaust and Hiroshima, we see daily news bulletins replete with violence, torture, hostilities, miscarriages of justice, genocide, bullying, and scapegoating. The details of the gospel story are particular, but the components of the tragedy are perennial. It is part universal story, part particular story. Jesus Christ focuses it, deepens it, sharpens it, yet it is also our story, and one that rings true to life. Thus it is both myth, in the technical sense of a transcendent, symbolic, unverifiable story that gives meaning to existence, and history, in the sense that the myth has intersected with the actual existence of a certain person on earth at a particular time in a particular place. The mythical element is precisely what makes it ring true. Factuality reduces it to just another vicious miscarriage of justice. Myth enables it to give hope and meaning to our lives. The association of Adam and Christ exposes the depths of the human predicament and the promise of its transformation. The Serpent-Christ epitomizes this, and here is my third poem.

The Healing Cross[17]

It

twists in the

heart

this worm of habit

that coils

around exuding its thoughts poisonous green

within the soul, warping the unwary

mind

and proving

the good that

I would

that I do

not. But

thanks be to

God!

The brazen antidote

injected into the veins

seeps secretly within the

soul—

the sting of the

serpent Christ—

it lowers the temperature, empties the feverish

self

and lifts the sights to a sign of peace and love

beyond imagination:

the healing cross.

Drama and Liturgy

To me it has become ironic that we are part of a culture where so much drama and fiction fills our lives, yet all we want is the facts. True, most drama and fiction nowadays is mere entertainment. A lot is not very profound and most consumers go for romance and happy endings, if not

17. The shape of this poem was suggested by the Serpent-Christ image on Mt. Nebo (Fig, 24).

outright comedy. But plenty enough is concerned with violence and crime, the triumph of good over evil, or its diabolical opposite, and science fiction projects such fundamental human concerns onto the skies. Indeed, our culture's impoverished literalism worries about whether violent film and video games breed violence in those addicted to watching or playing them. Maybe the addiction that demands ever more grotesque sensation does desensitize to the horrors; yet this is a far cry from the ancient perception that *katharsis* comes through tragic drama. *Katharsis* means purification and it is no accident that tragic drama emerged in classical Greece from religious rituals, nor that myths provided the storylines. The Greek philosopher Aristotle famously wrote that tragedy, through the arousal of pity and fear, effected the *katharsis* of such emotions.

But how? Well, let us recall our reference in chapter 2 to Mary Douglas' book *Purity and Danger*,[18] in which she explains how primitive peoples took things that were taboo, like blood and death, and by putting these fearful things into a ritual context, sacralized them. She used the analogy of turning weeds and lawn cuttings into compost to indicate how ritual could transform them from being life-denying to life-affirming. Thus, sacrifice turned blood into a means of purification. What was involved was a shift in perspective as the taboo subject was handled and faced and put into another context. By ritually killing an animal and surrounding this killing "with a ceremony indicative of the killers' innocence and their respect for life," the sacrificers both acknowledged and distanced themselves from their potential for violence.

Tragic drama most probably originated from sacrifice and works in the same kind of way: it makes it possible for human beings to avoid escapism, to confront things they dare not. By dramatic presentation we are enabled to face up to those things about the human condition we would rather forget or deny. Not for nothing did the great director Peter Brook suggests that there is "Holy Theatre":[19] "We are all aware that most of life escapes our senses. We know that the world of appearance is a crust—under the crust is the boiling matter we see if we peer into a volcano." So in theatre, the "invisible becomes visible"; we find liberation from our ordinary everyday selves. This is what makes "the theatre a holy place in which a greater reality could be found," often in the paradox of a loss which is also gain. Great tragedy probes for the meaning behind it all. It exposes the truth about the human condition so that it may be faced and ritually dealt with.

18. Douglas, *Purity and Danger*, especially 163ff.

19. Brook, *The Empty Space*, ch. 2.

So what I now want to suggest is that the cross functions like tragedy.[20] The drama exposes the reality of human sin, the insoluble conflicts that so often lead to the suffering of the innocent, the banishment and destruction of what is good, the mobilization of the political and religious structures to eliminate change or challenge. Christ is thrust outside the camp, banished like the scapegoat. All humanity is involved in the shame of it. Yet the story of the cross is redemptive. For the things we fear, the taboos of blood and death, the curse of the most cruel and despicable punishment devised by humanity, these are sacralized—put in a positive context in which they can be faced and dealt with. The drama effects an exposure of the truth. It becomes a universal narrative, a story told by an inspired poet, not a mere chronicler or historian. As Aristotle put it, "poetry is both more philosophical and more serious than history, since poetry speaks of universals, history of particulars." The terrible truth of human complicity in evil, of goodness snuffed out, of God's abandonment, is exposed and faced, faced as in a ritual context: the thing that is taboo is turned into something holy, the sin we cannot bear to face is redeemed, the pollution we usually fail to observe is revealed, and *katharsis*, in the sense of purification or atonement, is effected.

Now what this means, I suggest, is that the most effective *theōria* whereby we construe the cross must arise from participation in liturgy. It is in the *anamnēsis*, the re-presentation of the drama in the Eucharist, that we are enabled to "see through" to its meaning. This point was anticipated in the opening chapter. The *anamnēsis* of the Passover is what shapes the identity of Jews from generation to generation, reminding the community of its covenant with the God who liberated them from slavery in Egypt. For the earliest Christians this was the context that shaped their discernment of the significance of the cross. In the gathered community, the offering of the first-fruits of bread and wine and then the sharing of the gifts in communion draws the participants into the action, so that there is an instinctive "seeing through" to the "real presence" of the Christ who offered his body and blood for the salvation of the world. These signs of the cross are more than mere symbols—as Ephrem's Syriac word would indicate, they carry the power of the reality signified.

One thing worth noting here is the emphasis placed in chapter 2 on the deep connection of sacrifice with food, the stuff of life. Offerings, both in the Bible and in other sacrificing cultures, included grain, oil, olives, wine, even cheese, and animal sacrifices are only ever from domesticated herds

20. Previously discussed in *Arthur's Call*, chapter 5.

which might be used for meat, never wild or working animals—compare our culture's continuing resistance to horsemeat. From the beginning the Christian communion-rite was construed as first-fruits, a pure—indeed bloodless—sacrifice offered to the Creator in thanksgiving (hence "Eucharist," from the Greek for thanksgiving), then received again as spiritual food, the ordinary stuff of life becoming the stuff of eternal life. Gratitude for creation is found in many early sources, as is the sense that through eucharistic feeding we are assimilated to the new creation in Christ. Irenaeus, in particular, speaks of Christ giving directions to his disciples to offer to God the first-fruits of God's own created things: "he took bread," a part of creation, Irenaeus underlines, "and gave thanks, saying, 'This is my Body'"; then, goes on Irenaeus, the cup, likewise a part of that creation to which we belong, though given new meaning when Christ declared it to be his blood and the new oblation of the new covenant.[21]

> For as the bread, which is produced from the earth, when it receives the invocation of God, is no longer common bread but the Eucharist, consisting of two realities, the earthly and the heavenly, so also our bodies, when they receive the Eucharist, are no longer corruptible but have hope of eternal life.[22]

Thus, through the liturgy we give thanks for our creation, preservation, and all the blessings of this life, while also gaining *theōria*—a seeing through— to the life-giving renewal obtained by means of the offering of Christ's body and blood in death.

A second thing worth attending to here is the essentially practical way in which *theōria* is made possible. Studies of sacrifice have drawn attention to the fact that it is an action which does not encode a single, definitive meaning—indeed, participants may not have any conscious explanation of what they are doing. Yet they know what needs doing, and that things are better for doing it.[23] In a way, this challenges the long history of controversy over the meaning of the Eucharist, the Roman Catholic theory of transubstantiation spelt out in terms of a now-outdated philosophy of the way things are, the Protestant reduction of it to a mere symbol. The religious instinct that "sees through" the sacrament and receives new life from the liturgical *anamnēsis* of the cross as an offering of Christ's body and blood for the salvation of the world goes beyond the transactional and literalizing

21. *Haer.* 4.17.5.

22. *Haer.* 4.18.5.

23. See above chapter 2.

freeze that Reformation controversies introduced. Here is practical *theōria*, which discerns the drama as a whole, accepts the performative language of liturgy as not just remembering past action but with power effecting again what was done in the act commemorated.

If we take these points seriously, it may lead us to articulate what was done on the cross in a very different way. It is worth reminding ourselves of the power attributed to the Eucharist by the church fathers. Early on Ignatius spoke of the "medicine of immortality," and in chapter 3 we found this remarkable stanza from Ephrem's *Hymns on Paradise*:[24]

> The assembly of saints
>> bears resemblance to Paradise:
> in it each day is plucked.
>> the fruit of Him who gives life to all;
> in it, my brethren, is trodden
>> the cluster of grapes, to be the Medicine of Life.

Again, we briefly noted in chapter 1 how, in the christological controversies, Cyril of Alexandria was driven to defend his understanding of the incarnation because only this would guarantee the efficacy of the Eucharist. The holy body of Christ is life-giving, he suggests, when "mingled with our bodies" because it is united with the Word that is from God, and so with "the body of him who is life by nature" and "filled with his energy."[25] "When we taste of it we have life within ourselves, since we too are united with the flesh of the Saviour in the same way as that flesh is united with the Word that dwells within it." The Eucharist "will certainly transform those who partake of it and endow them with its own proper good, that is, immortality." It dispels both death and the diseases that are in us, for Christ comes as a doctor to tend us, his patients.

> It is as if one took the glowing ember and thrust it into a large pile of straw in order to preserve the vital nucleus of the fire. In the same way, our Lord Jesus Christ hides away life within us by means of his own flesh, and inserts immortality into us, like some vital nucleus that destroys every trace of corruption in us.[26]

The sheer physicality of this focus on the sacrament is striking—we receive divine life-giving energy into ourselves through actual eating of the bread,

---

24. *Hymns on Paradise* VI.8; Brock's translation.
25. *Comm. in Io.* 3.6 (on John 6:35), translated by Norman Russell.
26. *Comm. in Io.* 4.2 (on John 6:54), translated by Norman Russell.

which signifies the body of the incarnate Son of God. Maybe the cross should be construed as the life of God poured out for our consumption rather than in terms of sacrificial atoning death.

Which leads us to the question of blood. It is a conundrum that the symbolism of the Eucharist runs up against the biblical taboos on consuming blood, as John chapter 6 virtually acknowledges: the language of eating flesh and drinking blood, there attributed to Jesus, offends most of his audience, and they withdraw from him. Besides this, there is the issue of exactly what the word "blood" signifies in the Scriptures: as a student I long ago came face to face with the controversy then raging as to whether "blood" signified violent death or life. It is clear that statistically the word is used most commonly for death, of which "His blood be on us and on our children" (Matt 27:25) is just the most obvious example. On the other hand, Leviticus 17:11 is explicit: "For the life of the flesh is in the blood; and I have given it to you for making atonement for your lives on the altar; for as life it is the blood that makes atonement." What I suggest is that usage undermines this supposed binary opposition, "blood" ambiguously signifying *both* life *and* death, inasmuch as its substance holds the power of life whose very absence necessarily means death. That almost magical power makes it both taboo and sacred. In terms of Mary Douglas's analysis already outlined, the manipulation of blood in biblical sacrificial rites is what enables the community to deal with the life-denying anomalies of violence and death to which it is subject. Thus, blood becomes an agent of atonement, of purification and new life, a gift from God for the health of the community.

Furthermore, to minds shaped by biblical stories, the blood must have had what are called "apotropaeic" powers—bedaubed on doorpost and lintels, the blood of the Passover lamb protected the people from the Angel of Death. The Passover associations of the Eucharist probably made this meaning primary: one received the blood of Christ in the sacrament as a protective shield from the powers of sin and death. This notion that the cross was a protective shield was, I guess, pretty widespread. The signing of the cross on the forehead was undoubtedly meant to ward off evil powers, and when, as legend would have it, the true cross was discovered by Helena, mother of Constantine, she had the nails incorporated into a helmet and bridle bits to protect her son, the Emperor—a powerful kind of amulet. But surely there is more to it: the sacramental assimilation of the life-giving blood offered through Christ's sacrifice reinforces Ignatius' notion that the Eucharist is the "medicine of immortality, an antidote to death."

Thus, the "blood of Christ" coheres with the fundamental meaning traced throughout this consideration of the liturgy. By means of the practical action of communion in the body and blood of Christ, the cross is construed as a sacrifice by which violent death becomes the gift of life. So to my next poem:

Sacrifice

Except

a grain of wheat

fall to the earth

except

it be buried

or eaten

by a bird

except at harvest it be one among many grains

all winnowed, threshed and violently ground to flour

then kneaded and baked into bread, the staff of life

except

the lamb

be slaughtered

butchered

eaten

roasted

and shared

sacred blood

bedaubed

on doorpost

threshold

lintel

altar-horns

except

a life be

recycled

it fruitless

remains

surviving only if sacred in other life

if offered in sacrifice for life through death

The Cosmic Dimension

We have come right down to the everyday nitty gritty of food, the daily deaths on which our food consumption depends, and the re-cycling of life built into the very nature of our created existence. We have seen how the cross can be construed as a powerful symbolic representation of how death and life, natural and supernatural, are inseparable through the practical action of the communion-liturgy in which the first-fruits of life are offered and received. For Irenaeus this rooted the cross in creation, but not simply in a localized or particularized way. As we found in the first chapter, he conceived the cross as cosmic in its reach—the Son of God was visibly crucified on a cross with fourfold dimensions, embracing the dispersed from all sides, heights, depths, length, and breadth. Furthermore he suggested that it was on the same day on which Adam sinned that Christ died, recapitulating the death of all humanity and thereby granting humanity a second creation.[27] It is as if from the beginning the Creator of all bore the consequences of a creation in which there was potential for death as well as life. Thus, the cross cut across time and space, finding its location in God's eternal purposes, no mere remedy for an unfortunate accident within time, but a feature built into the very structure of the universe and a sign that "the Creator intended to use death creatively."[28]

It has often been observed that liturgical time is not the same as ordinary time. Ordinary time works with "before" and "after," in linear fashion; sacred time only knows the eternal "now."[29] In early Christianity the Pascha, celebrated in spring, quickly became a celebration of "the birthday of the cosmos," with the week of Christ's passion being a recapitulation of the week of creation. According to Blowers, the fathers

> frame the sacrifice of Christ within a panoramic, contemplative vision (*theōria*) of the drama of divine condescension in which God's very freedom to create the world in the first place, though unfathomable, is inseparable in human understanding from the "constraint" of the Creator's love and urgency to preserve and

27. *Haer.* V.23.2.

28. Blowers, *The Drama of the Divine Economy*, 263; see chapters 8 and 9 for fuller discussion.

29. This way of putting it reflects the way Sebastian Brock speaks of "the two times" in Ephrem's poetry; *The Luminous Eye*, 16.

renew the creation as creatures exercise their own freedom within the constraints of [creaturely] existence. . . . God created the world in order to sacrifice himself for it and thereby to bring it to perfection.[30]

Difficult though we may find all this, the famous depiction of the cross by Salvador Dali[31] perhaps enables us to break out of our scientifically in-formed realism about a universe more vast than we can imagine, and grasp something of the eternity of the cross in God's transcendent being and purposes. We are led back to where we began, the incomprehensible and the infinite, by our very earthing of the cross in the life-blood of creation. So to my final cruciform poem, inspired by everyday reality in parts of the African continent, by the way truths about life are veiled in the patterns of nature, pointing to the cross in creation and to Christ as the creative Word/ Logos in all things:

30. Blowers, *Drama*, p. 268.

31. Salvador Dali, *Christ of Saint John of the Cross*, oil on canvas, 1951. It can easily be found online.

An African Tree of Life

Along
the river
behind
the marshes
and reeds
mottled patterns of trees line the bank
skeleton trees, dead for winter, bare
arms extended grey-black, knotted with age
interspersed with occasional coloured shapes
leaves
retained
though dead
fire russet-red
others
conjure
dusty
grey-brown
earth, clay
vaguely vibrant
in evening light
masquerading
as blossoms
living death
yet unexpected
flowers turn
knob-thorn trees
to barely white
balloons
ahead
of leaves
and other bushes
delicately display
floating wings of
gossamer
purplish pink
and variegated greens
both dark and fresh
elusive hints of spring amongst the grey
promise life to come to the dry dead bush
when rains return and river floods well up.

A Final Word

The direction this journey has taken has caught me by surprise. Once I heard someone comment on the way we tend to put flowers on the cross, forgetting that it was probably the most cruel and sadistic form of public execution ever devised, especially given the slow and painful course by which death came to the victim. Many a time in the past I too have decried that kind of sentimentality. Furthermore, I have previously focused on the cross either as the Christian form of theodicy (dealing with the problem of suffering), or as the way of atonement (dealing with the problem of evil and sin). Yet this exploration of the types, signs, and symbols used for the cross by the early church has shifted the focus quite dramatically. It was not the suffering Christ they turned to, as people did in the Middle Ages. Nor was it the penalty of death for our sins they explored, as evangelicals do. Rather it was a quite paradoxical focus on life.

According to the New Testament "eternal life" is anticipated in the life we know on earth. For me as well as others, especially those in L'Arche communities, such life, at least in embryo, is experienced in what many would regard as "extremes," in being in relationship with those with profound learning disabilities, those who apparently live impoverished lives yet generate and share in the fruits of the Spirit, drawing others into community and communion through their vulnerability.[1] This paradoxical reality seems remarkably endorsed by the perception we have reached in this study—that life is found through acceptance of death as the way of new birth.

Here we have found that, whether construed as a sacrifice or as a gallows-tree, the cross paradoxically becomes a sign of life renewed. It is as though the fathers were "seeing through" death to life in all its fullness,

---

1. See further my book *Arthur's Call*, especially chapter 3.

and if that is what the cross is about—new life emerging paradoxically from death—then God's creative grace alone could effect it. It is no wonder that Ephrem could align Mary's womb with Sheol and Jordan.[2] Unlike theories, which purport to control and explain, such overlaying of images, along with metaphor, enigma, and paradox, can stimulate *theōria*, generating creative insights whereby to construe the cross, and this despite the "extremes" and the elusiveness. And thus is fed the fitting response of joy, thanksgiving, and praise. For "in my end is my beginning,"[3] and death proves to be birth to newness of life.

2. Brock, *The Luminous Eye*, 90–93.
3. T. S. Eliot, *The Four Quartets*, 204.

Bibliography

Texts and English Translations

Ambrose. *De Officiis*. Latin text: *CSEL*; ET: *NPNF*. (Abbreviated as *Off.*)

Apocrypha and Pseudepigrapha. Edited and translated by R. H. Charles. Oxford: Clarendon, 1913.

Apostolic Fathers. Greek text and ET: *The Apostolic Fathers*. Edited and translated by Kirsopp Lake, *LCL*. ET: *Early Christian Writings*. Edited by Maxwell Staniforth and Andrew Louth. Penguin Classics. London: Penguin, 1987.

Aristeas, Letter of, see *Apocrypha and Pseudepigrapha*.

Barnabas, Epistle of, see *Apostolic Fathers*. (Abbreviated as *Ep. Barn.*)

Basil of Caesarea. *On the Holy Spirit*. Greek text: *Basile de Césarée: Traité de Saint-Esprit*. Edited by B. Pruche, *SC*; ET: *NPNF* and *St. Basil the Great: On the Holy Spirit*. Translated by David Anderson. Crestwood, NY: St Vladimir's Seminary Press, 1980. (Abbreviated as *De Spir. S.*)

Basil of Caesarea. *Letters*. Greek Text and ET: *LCL*. (Abbreviated as *Ep.*)

Bonaventure. *The Soul's Journey into God, The Tree of Life, The Life of St. Francis*. Translated by Ewert Cousins. Classics of Western Spirituality. Mahwah, NJ: Paulist, 1978.

Cyril of Alexandria. *On Worship in Spirit and in Truth*. Greek text: Migne, *PG* 68.240–5; no ET available.

Cyril of Alexandria. Introduction and translated selections by Norman Russell. London: Routledge, 2000.

Diognetus, Epistle to, see *Apostolic Fathers*.

Ephrem. *St. Ephrem the Syrian, Hymns on Paradise*. Translated by Sebastian Brock. Crestwood, NY: St. Vladimir's Seminary Press, 1990. (Abbreviated as *HP*)

Eusebius of Caesarea. *Church History*. Greek text: *Die Kirchegeschichte: Eusebius Werke II*. Edited by E. Schwarz, *GCS*. ET: Eusebius, *The History of the Church*. Translated by G. A. Williamson. Penguin Classics. Harmondsworth, UK: Penguin, 1965. (Abbreviated as *Hist. eccl.*)

Gregory of Nazianzus. *Orations*. Greek text: Migne, *PG* 35 and vols. of *SC*. ET: *NPNF* and selections in *FC*. (Abbreviated as *Orat.*)

Gregory of Nyssa. *Contra Eunomium*. Greek text: *Gregorii Nysseni Opera*. Edited by W. Jaeger *et al.* Leiden: Brill, 1960–; ET in *NPNF*.

————. *The Great Catechism*: Greek text: *Gregorii Nysseni Opera*. Edited by W. Jaeger *et al.* Leiden: Brill, 1960–; ET: *The Catechetical Oration of Gregory of Nyssa*. Edited and translated by J. R. Srawley. London: SPCK, 1917.

Iamblichus. *De Mysteriis*. Greek text edited by G. Parthey. Berlin: 1857.

Ignatius, see *Apostolic Fathers*.

Irenaeus. *Against Heresies*. Greek text: *Irénée de Lyon: Contre les hérésies*. Edited and translated by A. Rousseau and L. Doutreleau, *SC*. ET: *ANCF* and *ACW*. (Abbreviated as *Haer.*)

————. *St. Irenaeus of Lyon, On the Apostolic Preaching*. Translated by John Behr. Crestwood, NY: St. Vladimir's Seminary Press, 1997. (Abbreviated as *Epid.*)

Julian of Norwich. *Julian of Norwich: Revelations of Divine Love*. Translated by Clifton Wolters. Penguin Classics. Harmondsworth, UK: Penguin, 1966.

Justin. *Dialogue with Trypho*. Greek text: *Dialogus cum Tryphone*. Edited by M. Markovich, *PTS*. ET: *FC*. (Abbreviated as *Dial.*)

Life of Adam and Eve, see *Apocrypha and Pseuepigrapha*.

Lucian. *On Sacrifices*. Greek text and ET: *LCL*. Edited by A. M. Harmon.

Melito. *Melito of Sardis, On Pascha and Fragments*. Greek text and English translation. Edited and translated by Stuart George Hall. Oxford Early Christian Texts. Oxford: Clarendon, 1979.

————. *Melito of Sardis. On Pascha* (with fragments and other material). Translated and annotated by Alistair Stewart-Sykes. Crestwood, NY: St Vladimir's Seminary Press, 2001. (Abbreviated as *PP*)

The Nag Hammadi Library in English. Translated by members of the Coptic Gnostic Library Project of the Institute for Antiquity and Christianity. Leiden: Brill, 1977.

Origen. *Contra Celsum*. Greek text: *Contre Celse: Introduction, Texte Critique, Traduction et notes*. Edited by M. Borret, *SC*. ET: *Contra Celsum*. Translated by Henry Chadwick. Cambridge: Cambridge University Press, 1980. (Abbreviated as *Cels.*)

————. *Homilies on Leviticus*. Greek text: Migne, *PG*. (Abbreviated as *Hom. Lev.*)

————. *On First Principals*. Greek text: *Origenes Werke*. Edited by P. Koetschau *et al.*, *GCS*. ET: *On First Principles*. Translated by G. W. Butterworth. 1936. Reprint. Eugene, OR: Wipf & Stock, 2012. (Abbreviated as *Princ.*)

Porphyry. *De Abstinentia*. Greek text: *Porphyrii Opuscula Selecta*. 2nd ed. Edited by A. Nauck. 1886. Reprint. Hildesheim, Germany: Olms, 1963.

Psalms of Solomon, see *Apocrypha and Pseudepigrapha*.

Socrates. *Church History*. Greek text: *GCS*; ET: *NPNF*.

Tertullian. *Adversus Marcionem*. Latin text: *CCL*; ET: *ANCL*. (Abbreviated as *Marc.*)

————. *De Praescriptione Haereticorum*. Latin text: *CCL*; ET: *ANCL*. (Abbreviated as *Praescr.*)

Theodoret of Cyrus. *Eranistes*. Greek text: *Eranistes*. Edited by Gerard H. Ettlinger. Oxford: Oxford University Press, 1975. ET: *NPNF*.

————. *The Questions on the Octoteuch. Vol. 1: On Genesis and Exodus*. Greek text edited by John F. Pettruccione and translated with introduction and commentary by Robert C. Hill. Library of Early Christianity vol. 1. Washington, DC: The Catholic University of America Press, 2007.

Secondary Literature

Anderson, Gary A. *The Genesis of Perfection: Adam and Eve in Jewish and Christian Imagination.* Louisville: Westminster John Knox, 2001.

Antonelli, Pierpaolo, and Paul Gifford, eds. *Can We Survive Our Origins? Readings in René Girard's Theory of Violence and the Sacred.* East Lansing, MI: Michigan State University Press, 2015.

Barrett, C. K. *The Gospel according to St. John.* 2nd ed. London: SPCK, 1978.

Birdsall, J. Neville, "Diatessaric Readings in the Marterdom of St Abo of Tiflis." In *New Testament Textual Criticism: Essays in Honour of Bruce M. Metzger*, edited by E. J. Epp and G. D. Fee, 313–24. Oxford: Oxford University Press, 1981.

Blowers, Paul M. *The Drama of the Divine Economy.* Oxford: Oxford University Press, 2012.

Brock, Sebastian. *The Luminous Eye: The Spiritual World Vision of St. Ephrem.* 1985. Reprint. Collegeville, MN: Cistercian, 1992.

Brook, Peter. *The Empty Space.* London: MacGibbon and Kee, 1968.

Burkitt, F. C. *Church and Gnosis.* Cambridge: Cambridge University Press, 1932.

Daniélou, J. *The Theology of Jewish Christianity.* London: DLT, 1964.

Douglas, Mary. *Leviticus as Literature.* Oxford: Oxford University Press, 1999.

———. *Purity and Danger.* London: Routledge and Kegan Paul, 1966.

Dunnill, John. *Sacrifice and the Body: Biblical Anthropology and Christian Self-Understanding.* Farnham, UK: Ashgate, 2013.

Fiddes, Paul S. *The Creative Suffering of God.* Oxford: Clarendon, 1988.

Eliot, T. S. *The Four Quartets: Collected Poems 1909–1962.* London: Faber and Faber, 1974.

George, Arthur, and Elena George. *The Mythology of Eden.* Lanham, MD: Hamilton, 2014.

Girard, René. *Deceit, Desire and the Novel: Self and Other in Literary Structure.* Translated by Y. Freccero. Baltimore: Johns Hopkins University Press 1965.

———. *I See Satan Fall like Lightning.* Translated by James G. Williams. Leominster, UK: Gracewing, 2001.

———. *The Scapegoat.* Translated by Y. Frecerro. Baltimore: Johns Hopkins University Press 1986.

———. *Violence and the Sacred.* Translated by P. Gregory. Baltimore: Johns Hopkins University Press 1977.

Goulder, Michael, ed. *Incarnation and Myth.* London: SCM, 1979.

Hansen, David. *Long Wandering Prayer: An Invitation to Walk with God.* Oxford: Bible Reading Fellowship, 2001.

Hick, John. *Evil and the Love of God.* London: Macmillan, 1966.

Jensen, Robin Margaret. *Understanding Early Christian Art.* London: Routledge, 2000.

Lanfer, Peter Thacker. *Remembering Eden: The Reception History of Genesis 3.22–24.* Oxford: Oxford University Press, 2012.

Louth, Andrew. *Early Christian Writings.* Penguin Classic. Harmondsworth, UK: Penguin, 1987.

MacKenzie, Iain M. *Irenaeus' Demonstration of the Apostolic Preaching: A Theological Commentary and Translation.* Aldershot, UK: Ashgate, 2002.

Messinger, Tryggve N. D. *The Eden Narrative: A Literary and Religio-Historical Study of Genesis 2–3.* Winona Lake, IN: Eisenbrauns, 2007.

Meszaros, Julia, and Johannes Zachhüber, eds. *Sacrifice and Modern Thought.* Oxford: Oxford University Press, 2013.

Moltmann, Jürgen. *The Crucified God: The Cross of Christ as the Foundation and Criticism of Christian Theology*. Translated by R. A. Wilson and John Bowden. London: SCM, 1974.

Murray, Robert. *Symbols of Church and Kingdom: A Study in Early Syriac Tradition*. Rev. ed. London: T. & T. Clark, 2004.

Noble, Thomas. *Holy Trinity, Holy People: The Theology of Christian Perfecting*. Didsbury Lectures. Eugene, OR: Cascade, 2013.

Nussbaum, Martha C. *The Fragility of Goodness: Luck and Ethics in Greek Tragedy and Philosophy*. Cambridge: Cambridge University Press, 1986.

Salonius, Pippa, and Andrea Worm, eds. *The Tree: Symbol, Allegory, and Mnemonic Device in Mediaeval Art and Thought*. Turnhout, Belgium: Brepols, 2014.

Sanders, E. P. *Paul and Palestinian Judaism*. London: SCM, 1977.

Snyder, Graydon F. *ANTE PACEM: Archaeological Evidence of Church Life before Constantine*. Macon, GA: Mercer University Press, 2003.

Stewart-Sykes, Alistair. *The Lamb's High Feast: Melito, Peri Pascha and the Quartodeciman Paschal Liturgy at Sardis*. Leiden: Brill, 1998.

Ullucci, Daniel C. *The Christian Rejection of Animal Sacrifice*. Oxford: Oxford University Press, 2012.

Williams, Rowan. *The Edge of Words: God and the Habits of Language*. London: Bloomsbury, 2014.

Young, Frances M. *Arthur's Call: A Journey of Faith in the Face of Severe Learning Disability*. London: SPCK, 2014.

———. *Can These Dry Bones Live? The Excitement of Theological Study*. 1982. Reprint. London: SCM, 1992.

———, with assistance from Arthur. *Face to Face*. London: Epworth, 1985.

———. *Face to Face: A Narrative Essay in the Theology of Suffering*. Edinburgh: T. & T. Clark, 1990.

———. *God's Presence: A Contemporary Recapitulation of Early Christianity*. Cambridge: Cambridge University Press 2013.

———. "The Idea of Sacrifice in Neoplatonic and Patristic Texts." *Studia Patristica* XI (1972) 278–81.

———. *The Making of the Creeds*. London: SCM, 1991.

———. "The Mark of the Nails." In *Resurrection: Essays in Honour of Leslie Houlden*, edited by Stephen Barton and Graham Stanton, 139–53. London: SPCK, 1994.

———. *Sacrifice and the Death of Christ*. 1975. Reprint. Eugene, OR: Wipf and Stock, 2009.

———. *Sacrificial Ideas in Greek Christian Writings from the New Testament to John Chrysostom*. Patristic Monograph Series no. 5. Cambridge, MA: Philadelphia Patristic Foundation, 1979.

General Index

Scripture Index

∾

APOCRYPHA & INTERTESTAMENTAL LITERATURE

∾

NEW TESTAMENT

Made in the USA
San Bernardino, CA
02 May 2019